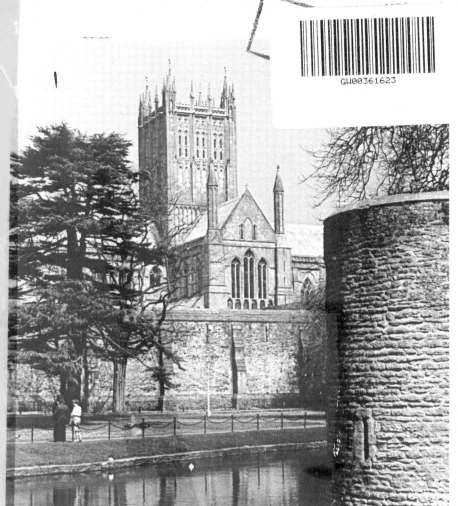

Wells Cathedral from across the moat of the Bishop's Palace.

Shire County Guide 1

SOMERSET

Martyn Brown

Shire Publications Ltd

CONTENTS

Printed in Great Britain by C. I. Thomas & Sons (Haverfordwest) Ltd, Press Buildings, Merlins Bridge, Haverfordwest, Dyfed SA61 1XF.

British Library Cataloguing in Publication Data: Brown, Martyn. *Somerset.* — 2nd ed. — (Shire County Guide;1). 1. Somerset — Visitors' guides. I. Title. 914. 23'804858. ISBN 0-85263-960-0.

ACKNOWLEDGEMENTS
The photograph on page 14 is reproduced by courtesy of Somerset County Museum. The map is by David R. Darton. All other photographs are by Cadbury Lamb.

Cover: *The village pond at East Quantoxhead.*

The Royal Oak at Winsford, the village where Ernest Bevin was born.

West Sedgemoor from Red Hill near Langport.

1

The regions of Somerset

Somerset is a county of rich variety. Within its borders can be found a microcosm of British landscape and geography. The Moors or Levels of central Somerset comprise one easily defined region; around that misty plain the land rises steeply on the eastern side with the sharp scarp of the Mendip Hills, more gently on the west towards the Quantock Ridge. To the south lies the gently rolling 'middle land' characteristic of this fertile agricultural county. The western boundary of Somerset splits the bare plateau of Exmoor just at the point where the wild Doones once rampaged at Badgworthy Water.

Somerset has never been a particularly popular county compared, say, with Devon or Cornwall. It has always been a region travellers passed through. Once stage coaches rattled down from London or Bristol to Exeter; today drivers tear past on the M5. They scarcely have time to glimpse the countryside around them that is waiting to be discovered.

In 1974 the reorganisation of the boundaries sliced off the more prosperous eastern portion of Somerset, including the largest city, Bath, and left a rural county. Taunton is the county town and the administrative centre of the county, with Yeovil and Bridgwater as the principal industrial towns, although neither bears the mark of heavy industry.

Somerset has remained remarkably unspoilt and is only slowly revealing its treasures now that tourism is seen as a path towards prosperity. Development has been limited to a narrow coastal fringe at Burnham-on-Sea and Minehead; inland, apart from the popular centres (Cheddar, Wells and Glastonbury particularly), many areas of outstanding natural beauty are deserted. Some of the smaller towns like Frome or Bruton, which once prospered with the woollen industry, have sadly decayed but are now making the most of their quaint charms. Exmoor perhaps is an exception, having always attracted visitors, and some of the most celebrated sites, like Tarr Steps or Exford, are suffering the effects of too many visitors.

3

Peat blocks drying on Sedgemoor.

Between the highlands that surround the county and the low Moors in the centre, the landscape of Somerset is gentle and wooded. It offers some of the richest agricultural land in Britain and is efficiently and intensively farmed. This area includes the fertile Vale of Taunton Deane and most of southern Somerset. Most of the county's large towns are in this region, each serving the surrounding agricultural community and acting as marketing, commercial and social centres. The overall impression, when travelling through this area, is of a green and pleasant land: small fields, neatly hedged with hawthorn, rich pastures with grazing cattle, golden corn and apple orchards.

In 1900 about 25,000 acres (10,000 ha) of the county were given over to cider apple orchards. Remnants of their gnarled trees can still be seen, but today dwarf trees, of new virus-resistant stock, are planted in formal and neat rows. At one time almost every farm had a cider press and every community, however small, a cider house where the local men could gather for a pint and a pipe. Cider has been made in Somerset for at least seven hundred years. In the eighteenth century it was described as 'strong, palatable and highly esteemed as a wholesome table liquor' and was even favourably compared with French wines. The method of making cider has scarcely changed at all since those days, although the scale of modern manufacture is very different, as are the standards of hygiene. Modern methods can be seen at Sheppy's cider factory

near Bradford-on-Tone or at Norton Fitzwarren, the home of the Taunton Cider Company. 'Scrumpy', or farmhouse cider, is made by some farmers still using the ancient apple mills and wooden cider presses bought by their grandfathers a hundred years ago.

The other well known product of the meadow land of Somerset is Cheddar cheese, made not only in Cheddar but throughout the county and in many other parts of the world. It was a Somerset man, Joseph Harding, who standardised the process of making Cheddar cheese in the 1860s. His sons emigrated to New Zealand at the end of the nineteenth century and took their knowledge of cheese-making with them, so although we may look down on the imported product, New Zealand Cheddar has a pedigree almost as well established as the true Somerset cheese. As early as 1086 cheeses from Somerset were highly valued. In 1625 the quality of cheeses from the district was recognised, and they were 'in such esteem at court that they are bespoken before they are made'.

THE MOORS

In other parts of Britain 'moorland' suggests an upland region, but in Somerset the Moors form the flat central core of the county, with land scarcely rising above sea level. In the past this area formed a boggy marsh covered by the sea at high tide. Since the middle ages, when the Abbot of Glastonbury, who owned the marshes, started to drain them, continuous improvements have been made so that now serious floods are a rare occurrence. Sometimes the Moor south of Burrow Mump (between Glastonbury and Taunton) is intentionally flooded in the winter to protect the young grass from frost and spread the rich alluvium over the fields. Then it is easy to imagine how the whole area must have appeared to Somerset's earliest inhabitants.

The iron age villages at Glastonbury and Meare were sited on the edge of the marsh and complete boats were retrieved during excavations, amazingly well preserved in the peat soil. Until quite recently every family living on the Moors had a primitive flat-bottomed boat tied up at the back door in case of emergency. An eighteenth-century writer described the area as 'much neglected, being destitute of gentlemen's houses, probably on account of the stagnant waters and unwholesome air'.

The landscape of the Moors is flat, monotonous to some eyes. The fields are bounded by deep ditches called 'rhines', often lined by willow trees. The willows have usually been pollarded, so a fat trunk about 8 feet (2.5 metres) high sports a spiky head-dress of new shoots. The cottages, houses or hamlets sit perched on slight rises in the land to save them from possible flooding. It is an extraordinary artificial landscape and the roads, following the line of the rhines, zigzag about with sharp right-angle bends and hump-backed bridges.

This damp low-lying area includes some 6000 acres (2400 ha) of peat moor. Peat, or turf as it is called locally, has been dug in Somerset since prehistoric times. Originally it was dug by hand for use as fuel, and even now there are a few hand diggers, but more recently machines have been used to excavate the peat for horticultural purposes. Across the Moors near Meare, Westhay and Catcott vast areas of peat have been exposed and dug out. Continuous pumping is required to reduce the water table and once the digging is completed and the pumping ceases long, narrow and deep trenches of black water are left to scar the landscape.

Around Athelney and Burrowbridge another unusual activity can be seen in the fields beside the main road. Here willows are grown as a crop for basket weavers. Somerset willows are highly rated and exported all over the world. When willow furniture was in fashion in the 1890s, over 2000 acres (800 ha) of the Moors were used for 'withy beds'. Since then the acreage has reduced considerably, but the method of cultivation remains unchanged. Locally grown willows have colourful names: Champion Rod, Black Spaniard, Long Skein, Blue Violet and Dicky Meadows. The willows are cut every spring at ground level from the 'stools' or 'stocks' from which they grow. Driving past in April or May, notice the bundles, or 'bolts', of withies gathered into heaps in the fields. The willows are processed at the grower's yard. Here the willows are sorted according to size. Some are stripped of their bark either in a machine or in a 'brake', others are boiled in huge tanks until the tannin in their bark turns them a golden brown. They can be seen lined up to dry against a fence or wall beside the road.

The Moors also provide rich grazing land for

Burrowbridge.

Above: *The beach at Kilve.*
Left: *Kilve: the oil retort house.*

cattle and sheep. Plans to lower the water table still further would allow the land to be ploughed, but conservationists claim that the Moors offer a vital and fragile habitat for many thousands of migrant geese and other birds. The water table forces many insects, worms and other creatures to the surface where they provide excellent meals for the migrants. If the water table were lowered these birds would have nowhere to feed.

THE QUANTOCKS

The Quantocks are a narrow range of hills running from just north of Taunton to the sea. Though they are a relatively minor geographical feature their character and vegetation distinguish them from the surrounding countryside. They are only 12 miles (19 km) long but give an impression of space and wilderness usually associated with a much larger landscape. The hills undulate softly, rising to a maximum height of 1260 feet (384 metres) at Will's Neck. The summits consist of heathery moorland with gorse thickets and bracken, virtually treeless except for an isolated holly or hawthorn and the occasional pine tree. The slopes and coombs, by contrast, are lush and green. Foxgloves and rhododendrons pack the banks of the swift streams. Sheep and ponies graze the moorland and the sloping fields, whilst red deer, fox and badger can be tracked along the rough paths and sometimes spied by a silent and careful stalker.

The Quantocks meet the sea at Kilve, where the cliffs fragment into almost regular blocks of stone as if hewn by the waves. Ammonites and other fossils can be found in the slate layers of the cliffs, and sometimes the remains of massive fossils create strange shapes in the shattered rocks that make up the beach. On the walk to the beach notice the ruins of the chantry founded in 1329 at the back of Priory Farm, and the more recent but equally interesting traditional low byre with round stone pillars on the other side of the track. There are also the remains of a lime kiln and buildings associated with an attempt to extract oil from shale early in the twentieth century.

The other village near the sea is East Quantoxhead, one of the most picturesque in the county, with a cluster of pretty cottages, a duck pond, farm, church and manor house. The Luttrells of Dunster have owned the manor since 1230. In the circular thatched building near the mill, a 'round house', a horse once turned a gear for driving an apple mill to make cider. In one of the cottages here a poor limbless girl was born to impoverished parents in 1784. She was called Sarah Biffen. Her parents sold her to a travelling fair and she was exhibited as a freak at Bartholomew Fair. She became quite famous as an artist, painting portraits of the gentry by clamping her paintbrush between her teeth. In 1821 she was awarded a medal by the Royal Society of Arts.

A local activity, now rarely practised, was the sport of glatting. A 'glat' is the local name for a conger eel. Down on the foreshore at Kilve conger eels, up to 10 feet (3 metres) long and with vicious teeth, live under rocks in the grey mud. In certain seasons, when the tide retreats further than usual after an exceptionally high tide the conger eels' hiding places are left exposed. A hunt used to be organised, with terriers and spaniels trained as 'fish dogs' and teams of men armed with heavy clubs. The 'field' would wade into the mud, lever up stones and hope to find and catch the congers amidst a flurry of flashing teeth and tails and flying mud.

A host of charming villages fringe the Quantock Hills: on the west side Bicknoller, Crowcombe, Flaxpool, West Bagborough and Cothelstone; and on the east side Holford, Nether Stowey, Spaxton, Enmore and Broomfield. Many of the churches contain superb examples of wood carving and are well worth a visit.

The magnificent walks up the coombs and over the wild summits, with views across the Bristol Channel and on either side across the landscape of Somerset, are the glory of the Quantocks.

THE MENDIP HILLS

The Mendip Hills form a natural barrier between Somerset and the new county of Avon. The sharp scarp of their western edge rises steeply from the low Moors. The Mendip plateau, rising to over 1000 feet (300 metres), presents an awesome prospect. The fields are divided by low dry stone walls. The soil is generally thin, so the pasture poor. It is always noticeably chillier up on the top than it is down below. Mendip is sheep country and the sheep are well suited to that environment.

The Mendips delight walkers and cavers. Beneath the landscape potholers manage to wriggle and squirm through black passages in the limestone mass to chance occasionally upon magnificent caverns. Some of these are open to the public, at Wookey Hole and Cheddar, where access is relatively easy. There are hundreds of holes all over the hills, but particularly around Priddy and Charterhouse. Walking through the fields one often comes across a pit with a hole at the bottom; fortunately there is usually a locked gate or door to prevent an unwary child or animal straying in too easily. Today caving is well organised and there are several clubs, often closely linked to one of the inns. Anyone wishing to explore a cave should report to the relevant club and seek advice. Never enter a cave alone or without informing the proper authorities.

The underground chambers are well matched by the splendid scenery above ground. Cheddar Gorge has become a nationally known attraction with concomitant ice cream parlours and amusements, while nearby Ebbor Gorge remains delightfully unspoilt.

Some of the most interesting archaeological remains in Somerset are to be found on the Mendips. Priddy Nine Barrows and Priddy Circles are fascinating places to visit, as is Charterhouse, where the Romans mined lead. In the nineteenth century a considerable industry developed up here. It was almost all short-lived; the remains of various mines, mills and workshops can still be seen. At Charterhouse there are some strange horizontal chimneys and massive cubes of waste from the lead mines. In the valleys near Mells a family of ironworkers, the Fussells, set up a number of workshops where iron was forged into scythes, sickles and billhooks, using water from the swift-flowing Mendip streams for power.

Those same streams were harnessed to drive the machinery in the woollen mills which brought prosperity to this area until the end of the eighteenth century. The small towns on the edge of the Mendips — Shepton Mallet, Frome and Bruton — all illustrate the decline that followed when competition from the north of England forced the local firms out of business.

The sheltered, south-facing slopes of the Mendip Hills, especially at Cheddar and Draycott, have become well known for their strawberries. It was not until the end of the nineteenth century that strawberries started to be cultivated on a large scale here, after a Cheddar man, Sam Spencer, started in the 1880s. Within a few years other market gardeners followed suit, taking advantage of the protective Mendips and the warm sunshine to encourage early crops. The value of the strawberries depended on getting them to market in prime condition, hence the Cheddar Valley railway became known as the 'Strawberry Special'. Railway wagons loaded with strawberries were attached to express passenger trains to London, Edinburgh, Glasgow and the Midlands. Although the railway line is now closed, strawberries are still an important local crop. More recently several vineyards producing English wine have been established here to take advantage of the soil and temperature conditions.

EXMOOR

The northern edge of Exmoor rises steeply from the sea to over 1500 feet (450 metres). The highest point, Dunkery Beacon, is 1705 feet (520 metres). Unlike other high moorland areas in the South-west, Exmoor is not a granite mass but is made up of sedimentary rocks, sandstones, slates and limestones. The best place to see the rock formations is at the coast between Baggy Point and Minehead.

The scenery of this region varies considerably: the valleys are deep, lush and richly wooded, the hilltops bare with coarse grass, heather, bracken and gorse. Wild as the landscape appears today, it has been dramatically altered by man over the centuries. As early as the thirteenth century the mineral wealth of Exmoor was being exploited and it continued to be until the end of the nineteenth century when the various workings became uneconomic. Veins of iron, copper and manganese traverse a belt of country from the Brendon Hills to the Simonsbath area; gold has been found in small quantities and silver-lead deposits were worked at Combe Martin (Devon). 270 pounds (122 kg) of Combe Martin silver were provided as a dowry for Edward I's daughter, Eleanor, upon her marriage to the Comte de Barre. Queen Victoria purchased brooches made of Exmoor silver in the nineteenth century.

The Royal Forest of Exmoor, the central and most barren part, was never wooded; the word 'forest' in this case is used in its medieval sense to mean an open hunting ground. Quiet walkers searching out the most isolated pathways can still be rewarded by the sight of a group of timid red deer. They have survived in large numbers and there are said to be as many deer in Somerset now as there were in the reign of Elizabeth I. Ironically, one probable reason for their survival is the continuing popularity of the stag hunt. A more familiar sight is the Exmoor pony, a tough stocky animal thought to be directly descended from the wild horses that survived the ice age. They have a thick undercoat of fine dense hair which enables them to withstand the harsh, bleak winter months.

In 1819 a pioneering farmer, John Knight, bought up 15,000 acres (6070 ha) of Exmoor Royal Forest, put a wall 52 miles (84 km) long around it, and, with the help of his sons, began to change the landscape by cultivating some of the land, farming sheep and cattle on most of it, building roads and homesteads and a large reservoir and leat. The remains of their handiwork can be seen in and around Simonsbath. One small farm, Pinkery, is now a County Educational Centre.

The Knight family's most dramatic visual contribution to the Exmoor landscape was the beech hedge. Massive hedges, now 15-20 feet (4-6 metres) high, were planted as windbreaks and shelters for cattle. Some of the saplings were set in earth between low double-skinned walls of herringbone-patterned stone, which can still be seen today. In 1841 Frederick Knight inherited the farm from his father and strove to continue their plans. He was still farming 9000 acres (3642 ha) when he died in 1897. He was knighted for his work in connection with the Volunteer Movement.

Another product of Exmoor which can still be enjoyed is the whortleberry. 'Urt' picking was a popular and profitable pastime for local children. Apparently Grabbist Hill, near Dunster, was where the first whorts ripened, but it was not a favourite place as they grew amongst gorse, so fingers and legs could be uncomfortably sore at the end of a day's picking. Fourpence a quart was paid at the beginning of the season — and it takes some time to pick that many!

The wilds of Exmoor live up to their reputation and despite the popularity of the area for holidays it is easy to escape the crowds and discover the peaceful atmosphere of the deserted moorland. Exmoor is popular with the naturalist, the walker, the huntsman, the fisherman (the Barle, the Exe and the West and East Lyn are excellent for salmon and trout and Clatworthy and Nutscale reservoirs are usually well stocked) and even the archaeologist. It is one of the rare open spaces where it is still possible to be alone.

Ebbor Gorge: the information shelter.

2
The countryside and coast

Ammerdown Nature Trail, near Kilmersdon (OS 183; ST 715534).

Starting from the Terry Hill crossroads on A362 between Radstock and Frome, this delightful nature trail winds its way through mixed woodland and eventually breaks out into the parkland belonging to Ammerdown House Field Study Centre, from which there are magnificent panoramic views across the Mendips. The walk takes about an hour, but there are short cuts for those not so energetic. A trail leaflet is available.

Black Rock Nature Trail, Cheddar Gorge (OS 182; ST 482545). Situated beside B3135 just above Cheddar Gorge.

Black Rock and Black Rock Drove nature reserves consist of 183 acres (74 ha) of rough grassland, plantation, natural woodland and scree at the head of Cheddar Gorge. There are two trails, one of 1 mile (1.6 km) and the other of 1½ miles (2.4 km), and they both provide good introductions to the natural history of the Mendip plateau and its characteristic flora and fauna as well as evidence of past human activity. The dry stone walling is typical of the area and has stood for two hundred years or more. Look out for interesting lichens growing on stones: one has been named locally 'Welcome-home-husband-though-never-so-drunk'.

Pass the old lime kiln in which the rock from the quarry was heated and used either as mortar for strengthening the walls or to spread on the land to replace lime lost through continual leaching of the thin soil. On a clear day you can see the North Devon coast to the west beyond Cheddar Gorge and, to the north, Black Down, the highest point on Mendip. On the skyline are several burial mounds and, in contrast, humps built during the Second World War to prevent enemy aircraft landing.

Brean Down, near Weston-super-Mare (OS 182; ST 290590). National Trust.

This 159 acre (64 ha) headland forms the south end of Weston Bay. Its prominent position commands extensive views up and down the coast, across the Bristol Channel to South Wales, and inland across the Levels to Glastonbury Tor. At the base of Brean Down is the Tropical Bird Garden (see chapter 9) and there is a disused Victorian barrack block on the top of the promontory.

Clatworthy Reservoir and Nature Trail, near Huish Champflower (OS 181; ST 040308).

A level leisurely walk 5½ miles (8 km) around the edge of this reservoir passes an iron age hillfort and through an area of ancient woodland. A leaflet about the nature trail, which forms part of this walk, is available from the tourist information centre, Taunton Library (see chapter 13).

CHAPTER 2

Draycott Sleights (OS 182; ST 483513). Access is from B3135 between Draycott and Priddy village.

The word 'sleights' is a local term for the sheep pasture provided by the rough limestone grassland on the Mendip scarp. The reserve is on the south-facing slope above the village of Draycott, with panoramic views across the Moors to Dorset, Exmoor and even South Wales. The reserve is particularly important for its butterflies, especially marbled whites, chalkhill blues and, occasionally, Adonis blues. There is an active badger set and a cave (access forbidden) where lesser horseshoe bats live.

Dundon Beacon (OS 182; ST 484326). About ½ mile (0.8 km) from the village of Compton Dundon off B3151 between Street and Somerton.

Although there are numerous footpaths around the beacon, a permit is required for the reserve, which occupies the whole area of the hill surmounted by a Celtic hillfort and bronze age cairn (the beacon). The permit can be obtained from Fyne Court, Broomfield, the headquarters of the Somerset Trust for Nature Conservation. It is worth getting permission, as the views from the top are very rewarding, extending across Sedgemoor to the west, where Monmouth's army was routed in 1685, and north towards Glastonbury Tor. The vegetation is varied, with ancient woodland of oak, hazel and field maple, and open downland with associated flora.

Dunkery Beacon. The car park is at OS 181; SS 904420.

The Beacon is the highest point in Somerset at 1704 feet (519 metres), with superb views over Exmoor and across to Wales. The walk to the summit is about ¾ mile (1.2 km) from the road, and there is a viewpoint indicator to identify features around. One of the finest walks is from Dunkery Gate (SS 895406), over the Beacon, and then down to the wooded valley below Cloutsham.

Ebbor Gorge National Nature Reserve, near Wookey (OS 182; ST 520485). Nature Conservancy Council and National Trust.

This enchanting woodland valley has similar scenery to Cheddar Gorge but on a smaller and wilder scale and without the crowds. Joints and fissures in the cliffs and bare rock faces hide hart's tongue ferns, butterflies, bats and badgers. The well marked walks start at the car park and lead down into the lush valley through ash, wych-elm, beech and oak woods. Look out for dog's mercury and enchanter's nightshade. A guide leaflet to the reserve can be purchased at the entrance.

Glastonbury Tor, Glastonbury (OS 182; ST 512386). National Trust.

No visit to Somerset is quite complete without making the pilgrimage up the steep slopes of Glastonbury Tor to the Perpendicular tower of the chapel of St Michael at the summit. The Tor can be approached from either side. The path from the main Glastonbury to Pilton road is the gentler climb, the northern slope somewhat steeper. The original chapel was destroyed by a landslip in 1271 and rebuilt in the fifteenth century. The tower is all that remains, with two sculptures above the west entrance, one of a woman milking a cow and the other of St Michael weighing souls. The views are superb in every direction and it is easy to imagine the importance of such a landmark in the days before proper routes were built across the dangerous marshes of the Levels below.

Ham Hill Country Park, Stoke-sub-Hamdon, near Yeovil (OS 193; ST 480168). 5 miles (8 km) west of Yeovil on A3088.

This well known beauty spot covering 154 acres (62 ha) overlooks the flood plain of the rivers Yeo and Parrett. There are extensive views in all directions, to the Mendips in the north-east, to the Quantocks in the north-west, and over the rolling Dorset countryside to the south. The park is set within the perimeter of the iron age hillfort and the huge undulations in the landscape are the result of quarrying for Ham stone, the warm golden stone used so extensively in this area and still being quarried today. There is a good picnic and parking area and toilets for the disabled. (See also chapter 3.)

Langford Heathfield Reserve (OS 181; ST 100235). About 2 miles (3.2 km) north of Wellington. Access from the Langford Bud-ville to Wiveliscombe road.

This is the largest area of lowland heath left in Somerset. The 180 acre (72.8 ha) site is valuable for the wild flora and fauna in a diversity of habitats. The common has been protected for hundreds of years as neither the owners of the land nor the commoners have been able to reclaim it for more intensive agricultural purposes. Bounded by oak and ash woodland, the sallow scrub and wet heath provide valuable breeding grounds for many birds, including tree pipits, greater and lesser spotted woodpeckers and grasshopper warblers, and for rare butterflies such as the brown hairstreak and the fritillaries.

Lydeard Hill, near West Bagborough, Taunton (OS 181; ST 180342). There is a car park and information board and marked walks are shown on a map.

This delightful spot situated in the heart of

10

the Quantocks offers superb views over the Vale of Taunton Deane to the south and is surrounded by the rolling farmland, wooded coombs and forestry plantations which typify the scenery of this part of Somerset. Throughout this region there are many lovely walks through unspoilt countryside dotted with attractive villages.

Ninesprings (OS 183; ST 558152). At the bottom of Hendford Hill, Yeovil, on A30.
There are 40 acres (16 ha) of woodland here, where over fifty species of wildlife have been recorded. Picnic areas, a nature trail and a children's play area are provided.

Somerset and North Devon Coast Path
A particularly impressive section of coastline can be found between Minehead and Hurlestone Point (now owned by the National Trust). It combines wild rugged cliffs with the rolling hills and coombs so characteristic of Exmoor. To the west lies the crescent-shaped shingle beach of Porlock Bay, while the other way leads towards Minehead and the fertile marshes around Dunster.

Steart Point (OS 182; ST 288472).
A spit of land on the west side of the Parrett estuary forms a nature reserve haven for migrating geese and wild fowl. It is a bleak spot bordered by mud flats of grey ooze extending as far as the eye can see across the Severn estuary to Wales. It is here, from the shingle ridge at Stolford, that the only surviving mud-horse fishermen of Somerset continue to use their traditional and unconventional mode of transport — a crude sledge which is pushed over the mud. As the tide retreats the fishermen go out to empty their nets set up a mile or more off shore. It is worth waiting for their return: fresh shrimps and rock salmon are their usual catch. Behind looms the bulk of Hinkley Point Power Station.

Velvet Bottom Nature Reserve (OS 182; ST 487549/503555). The upper end of the reserve adjoins the minor road from Charterhouse to Priddy and the lower end links with the Black Rock Nature Reserve.
This area is of special interest to those interested in archaeology as it passes through a now dry river valley where there has been extensive lead mining from pre-Roman times until the 1880s. The trail passes old slag heaps

and 'buddles', which are circular depressions about 23 feet (7 metres) in diameter, where the lead ore was washed out. Owing to the high lead content of the soil there is a notable sparsity of growth, with few trees except elder managing to establish themselves. There are some interesting plants particularly associated with lead, such as alpine penny-cress and spring sandwort. Towards the north of the reserve the flora and fauna become more characteristic of the limestone plateau of the Mendips. A trail leaflet is available.

West Mendip Way
This ancient trackway runs for about 30 miles (48 km) from Bleadon Hill near Weston-super-Mare (OS 182; ST 359579) across the Mendips to Wells. It follows footpaths, tracks and minor roads and can easily be picked up at many points along the route. It crosses many of the areas mentioned here, such as Black Rock and Draycott Sleights, passes Ebbor Gorge and descends near Wookey Hole.

West Sedgemoor Reserve (OS 193; ST 358238). RSPB. Forming part of the Somerset Levels, this reserve is entered off A378 from Taunton to Langport, 1 mile (1.6 km) east of Fivehead village.
There are low-lying wet meadows with intervening droves and ditches, bordered by deciduous woodland on the southern scarp. These are flooded in winter but dry out in spring to enable hay to be cut and subsequent cattle grazing. The reserve contains one of Britain's largest heronries, with about seventy nesting pairs. There is a hide from which they can be seen and a path across the moor with good views across the Levels. Look out for marsh marigolds, orchids and water violets in the dykes. A guide leaflet is available.

Wimbleball Lake (OS 181; SS 973319). About 1½ miles (2.4 km) east of Brompton Regis on a minor road between the village and B3190. The entrance to the nature reserve is at the bridge across the reservoir and there is general open access around it.
Picnic areas, woodland walks, car parks, a small camp site and a nature reserve surround Exmoor's 374 acre (150 ha) Wimbleball Lake Water Park, also noted as the premier trout fishing site in the South-west.

3
Places of archaeological interest

The following list of sites includes most of the more important sites where visible remains exist and to which the public has access (unless otherwise stated). Right of access should not be assumed and visitors should not disturb the sites.

PEAT TRACKWAYS

A unique record of life on the Somerset Levels from the fifth millennium BC to approximately AD 100 has been preserved in the peat moors, making them one of the most important archaeological areas in Europe. Because of the acid nature of the peat, and the absence of oxygen, organic materials such as wood, fibres and pollen have suffered little or no deterioration over thousands of years. Archaeologists have found marks on a piece of timber from a stone age adze as fresh as the day they were made, and a stone arrowhead still entwined with the gum and nettle fibre which bound it to a wooden shaft.

The reconstructed Sweet Track at the Peat Moors Visitor Centre.

Perhaps most exciting of all has been the exposure of the trackways: raised paths across the marshy Levels linking areas of higher ground. These originated 6000 years ago and became increasingly sophisticated in their timber and brushwood construction as time progressed. The trackways quickly disintegrate on exposure to the air unless they are specially treated and preserved, so they can be seen only in reconstructions.

On Shapwick Heath National Nature Reserve is the Sweet Track, the oldest wooden road in the world. It is now buried and preserved here but a reconstruction has been built at OS 182; ST 424408. Access is only from the north along an abandoned drive east of the Shapwick road. Enter the reserve along the signposted path to the reconstruction. At the Peat Moors Visitor Centre nearby there is another, smaller, reconstruction which visitors can walk along and an exhibition about the trackways (see chapter 9). The neolithic Abbot's Way track is reconstructed at OS 182; ST 419425 on B3151 near Burtle, behind Godwin's Peat Works.

STONE AGE

For most of the stone age men lived in small groups and survived by hunting and gathering plant food. In warmer periods they lived in small tent-like structures close to water, as the large number of stone handaxes found in the valley of the Broom near Chard suggests, and more recent evidence of habitation and activity around the Somerset Levels illustrates. In colder, glacial periods it was warmer to live in caves; both Cheddar Gorge and Wookey Hole caves reveal substantial evidence of this (see chapter 9).

BRONZE AGE

Metalworking was the major innovation of this period — first copper and later bronze. Initially metal was made on a small scale and possession of bronze tools and weapons must have been quite a status symbol. Round barrows, numerous on Exmoor and the Mendips, were built at this time as burial places. Standing stones, stone circles and the earthen circles at Priddy are all believed to have been used for ritual or ceremonial purposes.

Joaney How and Robin How (OS 181; SS 908428).

These two large circular burial cairns can be found on the north-east side of Dunkery Hill. They have not been excavated. Dunkery Beacon is the highest point on Exmoor at 1705 feet (520 metres) and well worth the climb for the splendid views across the Severn to Wales and east towards the Quantocks and Mendip Hills.

Porlock Stone Circle (OS 181; SS 846447).

This once impressive collection of ten standing stones and eleven recumbent ones in a circle about 80 feet (24 metres) in diameter was damaged during the Second World War. The circle is south of Porlock Common and is hidden from the road by a wall.

Priddy Circles (OS 182; ST 540527). Beside B3135 approximately 10 miles (16 km) east of Cheddar.

There are four circles, each about 200 yards (180 metres) in diameter, and with the faint line of an outer ditch. They belong to a group called henge monuments and may have been used for ceremonial events. Although they are on private property the owner has kindly agreed to allow access. Please remember to close the gate.

Priddy Nine Barrows (OS 182; ST 539515). Footpath from B3135 approximately 10 miles (16 km) east of Cheddar, just past minor road to Priddy.

One barrow produced cremated remains when it was opened in 1815. Today they form a most impressive skyline against the gentle green sward of this area of Mendip.

Robin Hood's Butts (OS 193; ST 230144 and 239129).

On the Blackdown Hills, this line of five round barrows, 60 to 90 feet (18 to 27 metres) in diameter, can easily be seen from B3170 south of Taunton.

IRON AGE

The introduction of iron smelting in this period allowed the production of much stronger tools. Defence was an important factor in the selection of settlement sites and the remains of many hillforts can be seen in Somerset. The lake villages of Meare and Glastonbury date from this period. Both have been extensively excavated, yielding fascinating evidence of the way of life of the inhabitants (see Somerset County Museum, Taunton, and the Glastonbury Lake Village Museum, chapter 8; and the Peat Moors Visitor Centre, chapter 9).

Bat's Castle (OS 181; SS 989421).

A hillfort with an almost circular enclosure overlooks the rushing tributary of the river Avill, just south of Dunster. It was once called Caesar's Camp, which complicates the story, as some of the ditches visible today

could date from the Civil War! The walk through Withycombe Hill Gate is pleasure enough, even if the origins of the structures are still obscure.

Brent Knoll (OS 182; ST 341510).

A natural outlier of the Mendips, which dominates the surrounding Moors of central Somerset, Brent Knoll cannot be missed as you drive down the M5. The site is superb, with views in every direction after an exhausting climb. There are numerous footpaths; try the one from East Brent, past the church.

Cow Castle (OS 180; SS 794374).

Local folklore says that this fortress was built by the fairies to protect themselves against the earth spirits. It is one of the most beautifully situated of all hillforts in this part of England. The best approach is along the footpath beside the river Barle, past the remains of the Wheal Eliza mine. There are well preserved entrances on the north-east and south-west sides.

Gallox Hill (OS 181; SS 984426). Situated above Dunster near A396.

Named after the gallows which formerly stood nearby, this is a small hillslope enclosure of less than 1 acre (0.4 ha).

Glastonbury Lake Village (OS 182; ST 493407). Down a minor road off B3151 between Glastonbury and Meare.

This is not an impressive site when compared with the wealth of material excavated. The only visible features are a few humps and bumps in a field. The discovery of the village in the 1890s was due to an amazing hunch by Dr Arthur Bulleid that there must have been settlements in this area comparable to similar lake dwellings in Switzerland. He travelled the area for months searching the fields for signs and one day noticed the humps that can be seen today.

Meare Lake Villages (OS 182; ST 443425).

On private land, the villages are visible from Meareway, a narrow public track.

South Cadbury (OS 183; SS 628252). Just outside the village of South Cadbury down a minor road from A303 between Sparkford and Wincanton.

A strategic site overlooking the principal routes to the West Country, it was occupied intermittently from neolithic times until the Saxon period. Most impressive are the bold ramparts of the iron age hillfort, once topped with elaborate timber fences to make an almost impregnable fortress. Over 18 acres (7 ha) are enclosed within the massive walls.

CHAPTER 3

ROMAN PERIOD

Apart from the superb mosaic from a villa at Low Ham and now in the County Museum, Somerset has disappointingly few remains of Roman activity.

Charterhouse (OS 172 or 182; ST 503558).

A Roman road crosses the Mendips to Charterhouse, about 5 miles (8 km) north-east of Cheddar and a mile south-west of B3134, where there were valuable silver and lead mines and a considerable settlement. You can see remnants of the mining (mostly nineteenth-century), a small amphitheatre and three rectangular enclosures. In Wells Museum there are four weighty lead bars, found near Charterhouse, presumably mislaid during transport.

Fosse Way

Parts of the modern A303 and A37 north and south of Ilchester follow the route of the Roman Fosse Way, the main road link from the south coast to the Midlands and eventually to Lincoln.

Ham Hill (OS 193; ST 483166). Beside the minor road from Stoke-sub-Hamdon to Montacute.

This huge L-shaped hillfort was occupied in the iron age, but the Romans mutilated the camp when quarrying for stone, creating the roller-coaster landscape you can explore to-day. Quarrying continues to the present day and throughout south-east Somerset you will notice the warm golden-yellow stone used for farm buildings and grand country mansions alike. Ham Hill is believed to be the only hillfort in Britain with an inn in the middle.

Ilchester (OS 183; ST 520226). Access via A303, which now bypasses the town, or B3151 from the north, or A37 from the south.

Somerset's principal Roman town, *Lindinis* was excavated in the 1970s. No remains survive above ground. There was a fort here in the first century AD, and a town grew up outside its walls. When the fort was disbanded the town continued to grow.

DARK AGES AND SAXON

Although many of Somerset's villages and small towns were founded during this period, little has been found to illuminate their history. A number of burials have been excavated and a few churches contain carved stones worked at this time.

Detail from the Low Ham mosaic in the Somerset County Museum, Taunton.

14

Tarr Steps.

Caratacus Stone (OS 181; SS 889337). Approximately 2 miles (3.2 km) south-west of Winsford, near Spire Cross.

The stone, erected in the sixth century, is inscribed CARATACI NEPUS ('nephew or kinsman of Caratacus') and is almost certainly a memorial stone. It is unlikely that it refers to the Caratacus who put up a stand against Rome from his headquarters in South Wales just after the conquest of AD 43. It has also been suggested that it guards a buried hoard of treasure, or that it marked the route from White Cross to Dulverton.

Ponter's Ball (OS 182; ST 531375). Just off A361 between Glastonbury and West Pennard.

A strange linear earthwork about 1 mile (1.6 km) long with a ditch on the east side. Its origin is obscure, but iron age pottery found in excavations suggests that it was a tribal boundary, possibly reused in the Dark Ages as an outer defence system surrounding Glastonbury Tor.

Tarr Steps (OS 181; SS 868321). 1½ miles (2.4 km) north of Hawkridge village.

Experts wrangle over the exact date of this superb clapper bridge over the river Barle. Seventeen spans of massive stone slabs form a structure 180 feet (55 metres) long. Teams of laden packhorses would have filed across the bridge, one after the other. Delightful walks follow the river to Withypool. Folklore tells that the bridge was built by the Devil. With his last load he tripped and broke his apron strings. The stones he was carrying fell at Mounsey Castle and Brewer's Castle not far away.

Glastonbury Tor.

4
Arthur and Alfred

Arthur is an enigmatic figure whose story is shrouded in such a tangle of history and folklore that it has become almost impossible to separate fact from fiction. His associations with the West Country are particularly strong, although every region of England, from the North to the tip of Cornwall, claims him.

Immediately after the withdrawal of the Roman armies early in the fifth century AD England was plunged into the Dark Ages. Some two hundred years elapsed before the Saxon invasions seriously affected much of Wessex, giving rise to the assumption that a powerful leader or chieftain, or a series of powerful leaders, took command of the West Country and held the invaders at bay. Arthur, it is thought, may be the generic term or popular name for that leader.

Archaeological excavations at South Cadbury have shown that the iron age hillfort was reoccupied in the late fifth or early sixth century AD and massive wooden fortifications were added to the ramparts. Foundations of an impressive hall were discovered, appropriate to a Dark Age chieftain. The site was large enough to accommodate an army of a thousand men. It is therefore possible that in this western frontier zone between Wessex and the squabbling Celtic kingdoms there was a great military leader who gathered about him a large band of followers and who moved widely about Britain fighting the Saxons. There are records of twelve great battles at about this time, the final one taking place at Mount Badon, which was possibly somewhere near Bath although the exact location is unclear, and it is widely assumed that it was Arthur, the legendary folk-hero, who defeated the invaders.

Sometime later, at the battle of Camlan, Geoffrey of Monmouth recounts that Arthur was mortally wounded and taken to the Isle of Avalon (Glastonbury), where, before he died, he threw his famous sword, Excalibur, into water now claimed to be near the bridge over the river Brue between Glastonbury and Street. Following the death of her husband, Queen Guinevere fled to Amesbury, where she took the veil and became abbess of the great abbey; after her death, her body was taken to Glastonbury by Sir Lancelot to be buried beside Arthur.

In 1184 Glastonbury Abbey suffered a disastrous fire; seven years later, on the instruction of King Henry II, the monks began to excavate the remains and found a tomb. On it was a lead cross inscribed, according to Camden's *Britannia* (1610), with the words 'Here lies the famous king, Arturius, buried in the Isle of Avalon'. Whether this is clear evidence of the existence and demise of King Arthur or merely a clever ploy to revive interest in the abbey as a place of pilgrimage, we shall probably never know.

Alfred came to the throne in AD 871 and is remembered by a memorial in Winchester as the 'founder of the English nation', a well deserved epithet for the great king who had

16

not only a major religious and military influence but who also pioneered tremendous progress in the field of learning. He personally instigated the translation of several classical books into Anglo-Saxon, so that his subjects could improve their education.

Although the majority of his activities took place in Wiltshire and Dorset, his Somerset associations are particularly important; the marshy swamps of central Somerset provided a safe haven and retreat for Alfred after a surprise attack by the Danes at Chippenham in AD 878. It was in Somerset that the great king sought refuge in a peasant's cottage and reputedly dozed while the cakes burnt. After seven weeks in hiding Alfred did, however, manage to defeat the Danes at Ethandun (Edington), Wiltshire. An uninspiring obelisk in a field by the A361 at Athelney marks the site where he later established a priory to commemorate his victory, but it was overshadowed by nearby Glastonbury and failed to prosper. After the battle Alfred brought Guthrum, the Danish leader, and thirty other Danes to Christian baptism at Aller, 4 miles (6.4 km) east of Athelney. Then the journey was made to Wedmore, the site of a royal residence, where a peace agreement was signed, separating Alfred's kingdom from the Danelaw of eastern England.

Alfred was still under threat from attack by other invaders and therefore arranged for additional fortifications at strategic sites around his kingdom. At South Cadbury he strengthened the ancient hillfort and in times of emergency the fortress was garrisoned by local men in great numbers — one man for every 4 feet (1.2 metres) of wall.

The Alfred Jewel, a masterpiece of Saxon craftsmanship inscribed 'Alfred had me made', was found at Parker's Field, North Petherton, in 1693. It is now in the Ashmolean Museum, Oxford, but replicas can be seen in the County Museum, Taunton, and the Glastonbury Lake Village Museum. More recently, at Cheddar, a royal residence has been excavated which was in use in the ninth century, possibly by Alfred. It included a hall 76 feet (23.1 metres) long, with a private chamber for the king or chief official. The outlines of the buildings have been marked out in the grounds of the Kings of Wessex School.

By the time of his death in 901, when he was in his early fifties, Alfred's kingdom of Wessex comprised all of England south of the Thames, and his son, Edward the Elder, continued to expand the boundaries of the realm. In addition he was responsible for creating the diocese of Wells, and it was at this time that the cathedral of St Andrew was founded (see chapter 6).

The ruins of Glastonbury Abbey.

5
Castles and monastic ruins

Castle Neroche, near Broadway, Illminster. Forestry Commission.

The ruins of his huge Norman defensive work dominate the area from its strategic position on the eastern edge of the Blackdown Hills. The castle is now approached along an excellent 2 mile (3.2 km) trail through varied woodland, and from the castle there are superb views of Taunton Deane and the Quantocks. There is also a good picnic area and car park.

Cleeve Abbey, Washford TA23 0PS. English Heritage.

The Cistercians usually chose a beautiful setting for their monastic sites and this is no exception. Over the gatehouse the Latin inscription means 'Gate, stand open, nor be shut to any honest man.'

The abbey was founded in the twelfth century and dissolved in 1537. The surviving buildings re-create a rare impression of what life must have been like in a medieval monastery. In the thirteenth century Henry III granted the abbey 'right of wreck' as parts of its estates bordered the Severn estuary and the

Cleeve Abbey gateway.

bits and pieces washed ashore by the tide on that windswept coast added to its prosperity. Frescoes (sadly faded and decayed) of St Thecla, St Margaret and St Katharine can be seen in the buttery, near the refectory. Look out, too, for the intricately decorated encaustic floor tiles.

Dunster Castle, Dunster, near Minehead TA24 6SL. Telephone: 0643 821314. National Trust.

The home of the Luttrell family for six hundred years, the castle dominates the surrounding countryside and coastal plain as well as the delightful medieval High Street of Dunster itself, with its octagonal market cross and yarn market.

The castle was granted to the Mohuns by William the Conqueror shortly after the Conquest and the gateway they built remains little altered to this day. In 1376 the castle was bought from them by Lady Elizabeth Luttrell for 5000 marks. During the Civil War the castle was besieged first by the Royalists and later by the Parliamentarians, after which most of the fortifications were demolished. The living quarters of the castle were altered and remodelled by Anthony Salvin (the architect of Windsor Castle) in the second half of the nineteenth century and he created its present picturesque silhouette.

The stables are early seventeenth-century with mullioned windows and complete with original boxes, now imaginatively converted into a National Trust shop.

Terraced gardens of subtropical plants have been created in the castle's grounds, with spectacular views over the surrounding countryside.

Farleigh Castle, Farleigh Hungerford, near Bradford-on-Avon BA3 6RS.

In its heyday the castle must have been an impressive stronghold, for it was of the type that combined strength with architectural order. It was built sometime between 1369 and 1383, having a rectangular inner bailey some 200 feet (65 metres) across, with four circular towers at the corners and a big gatehouse with two semicircular projections on the least protected south side. The outer bailey was added to this side in about 1425. All that remains today is two ruined towers and exposed foundations, which trace the past greatness and splendour. The Priest's House, built in 1430 and extended in the late seventeenth century, now houses a small museum with items relating to the castle and its history, including some fine stone carvings and samples

The Abbot's Kitchen, Glastonbury Abbey.   *Nunney Castle.*

of pottery. The chapel contains the fine tomb of Sir Thomas Hungerford, builder of the castle (see chapter 6.)

Glastonbury Abbey, Glastonbury BA6 9EL.
About 150,000 people visit these ruins each year. They are attracted not so much by the stones themselves, but by their setting and the legends and history that surround them. Legend links Joseph of Arimathea with Glastonbury. It is said that he travelled here after the Crucifixion and that from his staff grew the first 'holy' thorn on Weary-all Hill. There is a 'holy' thorn inside the abbey precincts today. King Arthur is said to have been buried here, with his consort, Queen Guinevere, and the site of his tomb is marked with a plaque.
The best preserved of the abbey's buildings is the kitchen, a square building with massive fireplaces and chimneys in each corner. The flues were carried up outside the vaulted central space to the lantern on the roof. It was probably built by Abbot Walter Monington between 1342 and 1375 together with the abbot's quarters, hall, chambers, chapel, larder and granary. The records show that the meals cooked here were not so gross as might be imagined. The monastery was organised under the rule of St Benedict, so one meal a day was the custom, of plain food with plenty of bread and a pint of wine.
In its heyday Glastonbury Abbey was fabulously wealthy and owned large areas of Somerset and surrounding counties. Some of its properties can be seen in the town and nearby villages: St Michael's Chapel on the Tor; the Abbey Barn, now the Somerset Rural Life Museum; the Tribunal; the Abbot's Fish House in Meare and the adjoining Abbot's Lodging; and other barns at Pilton and Doulting, now privately owned.

Muchelney Abbey, Muchelney, near Langport TA10 0DQ. English Heritage.
Unfortunately little remains of this tenth-century Benedictine abbey, Somerset's second oldest religious foundation: the monks first established themselves here in the eighth century. The fifteenth-century south cloister range and the abbot's lodging (once used as a farmhouse) are well preserved. Opposite the ruins notice the Priest's House (National Trust); this is a rare survival of a fourteenth-century house scarcely altered after six hundred years. Access to the house is restricted and is available only with written permission from the tenant.

Nunney Castle, Nunney, near Frome. English Heritage.

The castle is neither large nor commanding, but the tranquil setting and the strict symmetry of design are both enormously pleasing. There is a moat all round, fed by a stream. The castle was built in the French style, with a central oblong plan and a tower at each corner, by John de la Mare, reputedly from profits he made at war. He received a licence to crenellate it in 1373. It was ruined during the Civil War when a Parliamentary force, well equipped with artillery, bombarded it to surrender. The Roundheads tore out all the joists and floorboards so systematically that the place was never lived in again, although the exterior is remarkably complete.

Stoke-sub-Hamdon Priory, Stoke-sub-Hamdon, near Montacute TA14 6QP. National Trust.

Situated in the village, the fourteenth- and fifteenth-century buildings of Ham stone were formerly the residence of the priests of the chantry of St Nicholas. The great hall and screens passage of the chantry house can be visited and the magnificent thatched barn forms an idyllic backdrop to the farmyard.

Taunton Castle, Castle Green, Taunton TA1 4AA. Somerset County Council and Somerset Archaeological and Natural History Society.

Situated in the centre of Somerset's county town, Taunton Castle now houses part of the Somerset County Museum, having been saved from possible destruction in 1873 by the Somerset Archaeological Society. The first known fortress on the site was destroyed in AD 722 but was replaced by another before the Norman Conquest. In 1138 a huge square keep was built, and the only remaining area of the base section now forms part of the garden of the Castle Hotel. A cobbled roadway leads under the thirteenth-century gateway, which still bears the groove which housed the medieval portcullis. In 1218-19 the castle was extended to include the whole of what is now the Castle Green car park, and many of the present buildings date from an extensive rebuilding programme undertaken by Bishop William Ralegh in 1245-9. (See also the County Museum, chapter 8.)

The gateway to Taunton Castle.

The tower of Evercreech church.

6
Churches

The outstanding features of many of the parish churches of Somerset are the intricately decorated towers dating from the fifteenth and sixteenth centuries, at the height of the county's prosperity with the wool trade, and the unusual survival of a large number of medieval carved bench ends. The following list draws attention to some of the most significant buildings, but in no way does it attempt to be comprehensive.

Bishop's Lydeard: Blessed Virgin Mary.

Built of local red sandstone in the late fourteenth and early fifteenth centuries, the fine tower with pierced tracery battlements and pinnacles forms a dominant feature in the landscape. Inside the church are some interesting examples of early sixteenth-century carved bench ends, including a medieval windmill and a ship, and a wonderful fan-vaulted screen dating from the same period. In the churchyard there is a well preserved fourteenth-century cross, one of the finest left in England. One of the steps is hollowed out for alms or holy water and the twelve apostles are sculptured around the base, with Christ risen and enthroned. Close by are the remains of an earlier village cross.

Brushford: St Nicholas.

Beside the church stands a magnificent oak tree, probably some eight hundred years old, and it is amazing to think that this tree was here when the thirteenth-century church was built. The church pews were cut from other oaks over five hundred years ago, when the massive screen was also made, beautifully carved with fan-vaulting and an unusual feature for this area. There is an Edward Burne-Jones window, and a modern chapel designed by Edwin Lutyens, with a memorial to Aubrey Herbert, the traveller and diplomat upon whom John Buchan's 'Greenmantle' was based.

Crewkerne: St Bartholomew.

This is one of the finest fifteenth-century cruciform churches in Somerset, with a west front worthy of a cathedral. It is approached through a Tudor gateway flanked by tall gargoyled turrets. A golden cockerel surmounts the lofty pinnacles of the fifteenth-century tower. The south porch is decorated with carvings of a medieval orchestra, delicate figures playing their lyres, tambourines, harp and bagpipes beneath the beautiful stone vaulting of the roof. The interior is not quite so splendid, although there is a fine Norman font and the roof of the nave rests on thirteen great stone corbels carved as angels.

Culbone: St Beuno.

Why anyone should have chosen such a remote spot to build a church is hard to imagine, but the walk to it from Porlock, or from the little gatehouse at Ashley Combe, is beautiful. The path winds gently through woodland and fern-covered banks for 1½ miles (2.4 km) with the massive Exmoor hills rising steeply 800 feet (250 metres) high on the left-hand side. Locals claim that the church is the smallest in England: only 33 feet (10 metres) long, by 12 feet 8 inches (3.8 metres) wide. It has a porch, nave, carved oak chancel screen, Norman font and a slender slate spire. It is so deeply hidden in its narrow valley that the sun's rays touch the church for only four months of the year.

Downside Abbey, Stratton-on-the-Fosse.

The present Benedictine community at Downside dates from 1814. It was founded by the monks driven from Douai in 1793 by the French Revolution, but it was not until 1872 that a large programme of building works was undertaken, which included the plans for a church on the present scale, with a high spire. Only part of the abbey building was undertaken at this time. The north transept was started, with extremely ornate decoration inside, thick naturalistic capitals and rich carvings. Externally it is essentially Early English in style, with a big rose window and side aisles. Dating from this time also are the opposite transept and the lower section of the tower, and at the east end there is a magnificent French-style ambulatory with radiating chapels, finished in about 1890.

The church did not achieve its present cathedral-like splendour until early in the twentieth century. It is some 328 feet (100 metres) long and 74 feet (22.5 metres) high and creates an impression of great light and space. There are eleven bays, each with two double arches, and a dignified angel presides over each pillar in the lofty nave. The roof is vaulted, with finely carved bosses.

East Coker: St Michael.

'In my beginning is my end, ...In my end is my beginning' wrote T. S. Eliot, whose family can be traced in the parish registers of East Coker from the 1560s, when records began, and whose ashes are buried here. The main body of the church is Norman, with medieval additions, and a curiously placed tower was erected at the east end in the eighteenth century. Although Eliot never lived in the village he was drawn by its strong family associations and always found a deep peace and tranquillity in the mellow surroundings of the sleepy village.

In contrast, one inhabitant of East Coker was spurred to a life of adventure and exploration. William Dampier (1651-1715) is reputed to have been the first Englishman to set foot in Australia (in 1688). He circumnavigated the world three times and on one of his trips was responsible for piloting the ship that brought Robinson Crusoe home. There is a commemorative plaque to Dampier on the wall of the church.

East Quantoxhead: Blessed Virgin Mary.

This tiny church, situated in the picturesque village of East Quantoxhead, is approached up a path beside the outbuildings of a farm. It contains an Elizabethan pulpit with leaf carvings and beautiful bench ends decorated with berries, leaves and thistles.

Evercreech: St Peter.

The church, famous for its richly carved tower, stands on a green sward surrounded by grey buildings. It is a fine example of the Perpendicular style of church building so predominant in this part of England and has magnificent ornate parapets and gargoyles. The chancel is all that remains of an earlier building and the only later addition has been the south aisle of 1843. Inside it is unique among Mendip churches in that it has retained its north and south galleries, complete with numbered box pews. The overall effect is one of great light, height and airiness, enhanced by the brightly painted roof.

Farleigh Hungerford: Chapel of St Leonard, Farleigh Castle.

Originally the parish church of St Leonard, it was included within the outer walls of the castle in the mid 1420s and became the castle chapel. The present building dates from the mid fourteenth century, and the west door and window are probably original. The battlemented retaining wall now surrounding it is of nineteenth-century origin, but the early simple form of the plain rectangular building with diagonal buttresses at each corner can still be seen. The font is thought to be from the original church on this site, dating from the late twelfth century.

In 1844, after some plaster came away on the east wall, some beautiful paintings were discovered. These are thought to have been executed in the fifteenth century, possibly at the time when the castle took over the chapel. St George is depicted slaying the dragon, although now, sadly, the dragon is barely visible, and there are other figures, surrounded by a conventional pattern typical of

that time. Within the chapel are several tombs, including that of Sir Thomas Hungerford, the builder of the castle, who died in 1398, and his wife, who died in 1412. Tombs of later custodians of the castle include superb marble effigies from the mid seventeenth century, some of the finest in the country. On the altar is a black Bible printed in 1611, and one of a small edition in which there is the variant reading 'he' for 'she' in Ruth 3, 15.

Frome: St John the Baptist.

The first church on this site was established by St Aldhelm in about AD 685, but by 1170 it had been remodelled and replaced by the existing church, which exhibits a hotchpotch of styles from the twelfth century to the mid nineteenth century.

Approaching the church up the steps from the top of Cheap Street affords a good view of the Via Crucis, which leads up to the north porch. This is an unusual feature in an English churchyard and was designed and erected by Forsyth in 1866. It depicts six episodes on Christ's road to Calvary, with the seventh, the Crucifixion, above the north porch. The west front was remodelled three times in the nineteenth century, but it retains its basic fifteenth-century plan with the central door flanked by two sides portals which give access to the aisles.

Inside, the most interesting features are the thirteenth-century font, of quatrefoil design although much restored and altered, and the fine twelfth-century archway into the Cabel Chapel. The hammerbeam roof of the chancel is worth noting. With its carved wooden angels, it is a fine example of Victorian joinery. Two Saxon stones are built into the wall on the right of the entrance to the nave from the tower. The top carving shows two dragonesque serpents typical of the intertwining motif much loved by the Saxons. The lower panel depicts a galloping animal with a long swirling tail. It is thought to be part of a Saxon cross, placed here by the monks when they bore the body of St Aldhelm back to Malmesbury Abbey from Shepton Mallet, where he died in AD 709.

Ilminster: St Mary the Virgin.

This fine Perpendicular church is a fitting memorial to the town's prosperity in the fourteenth and fifteenth centuries. Built in 1450, the nave was largely reconstructed in 1825. The magnificent tower, the envy of many a surrounding parish, was copied from the central tower at Wells Cathedral, with 24 pierced stone windows to let out the sound of the bells, 22 pinnacles at the top and, rising above all that, a canopied stair turret with sixteen gargoyles. The transepts have impressive windows and niched buttresses, with a parapet of intricately carved gargoyles at the top. The roof of the tower is finely fan-vaulted, but unfortunately the inside was much spoilt by the well intentioned restorers of the nineteenth century and much of the beauty of the nave has been lost. There are some very good brasses here, notably those of Nicholas Wadham, the founder of Wadham College, Oxford, and his wife, Dorothy, in the north transept near the grave of their ancestor, William Wadham, who was responsible for financing much of the church building work.

Leigh-on-Mendip: St Giles.

The Perpendicular church tower, tall and striking, with its richly ornamented crown and triple windows, dominates the village, and the body of the church appears disproportionately small in comparison. The tower has an amazing 64 pinnacles and is decorated with oyster shells between the stonework. Externally, around the walls of the aisles there are open parapets with great bands of quatrefoils carved with roses and shields; it is no wonder that the masons thought it wise for their magnificent building to be guarded by eight huge gargoyles. Inside the imbalance of scale is not so noticeable, as the overall effect is one of spaciousness, with a west window of fifteenth-century stained glass. The roofs are beautifully carved: the chancel roof is of chestnut (which is reputed to keep the spiders at bay!) with fine oak panels and a cornice of oak angels, and the whole roof is supported by thirty stone angels. The font is Norman, the only reminder of an earlier church on this site.

Mells: St Andrew.

Situated in one of the prettiest and largest Mendip villages, the parish church is a superb Perpendicular building, with triple-windowed tower, similar to that at Leigh but even loftier, with blind tracery and pierced stonework. There is a fine fan-vaulted porch and a two-storeyed vestry, once a chapel, dated 1485. The extensive Victorian restoration of the interior managed to maintain the simple elegance of the original. The carved pew ends are examples of local craftsmanship, made in the village between 1860 and 1880. A surprising number of famous people contributed to the adornment of the church. The fine carved peacock is by Edward Burne-Jones and the large statue in the Horner Chapel, of Edward Horner mounted on horseback, was designed by Alfred Munnings, the pedestal by Edwin Lutyens. Notice also in this little chapel the lovely roof, with 96 oak panels and floral bosses, resting on stone angels.

The churchyard borders on the high-walled gardens of the Horner estate of Little Jack Horner's family.

Norton Fitzwarren: All Saints.

The magnificent chancel screen in this four-teenth-century church depicts a fearsome dragon creeping up on unwary villagers as they go about their daily tasks. Men crouch behind great bracken leaves and a second dragon stalks a group of men and dogs. Legend has it that after a battle at the local hillfort the anger of the dragon was aroused and he left his lair to prowl the village.

Othery: St Michael.

Standing high on a ridge in the middle of Sedgemoor, the cottages cluster around the church beyond the reach of the ever threatening floods. The church grew from Norman foundations with additions made until the fifteenth century. On the eastern gable is a cross, thought to be Norman. The font is fourteenth-century, and the tower fifteenth, whilst the beautiful carved door with a key

The church of St Mary Magdalene, Taunton.

23

over a foot long has Tudor roses in its tracery. The bishop's chair in the chancel is made from the old rood screen and bears a carving of a pelican and her young. There are splendid examples of medieval bench ends carved with flowers, butterflies and many remarkably fine figures such as David playing his harp, a soldier bearing the head of John the Baptist and a knight and his lady. Perhaps the most precious treasure in the church is part of a fifteenth-century cope showing beautiful medieval embroidery depicting the Madonna rising to heaven.

Shepton Mallet: St Peter and St Paul.

Rising high above the town is the first of the famous Somerset towers, the forerunner of a tradition which has become the county's landmark. It is a bold structure, with pinnacled buttresses and immense gargoyles, capped by the stump of a little spire which it appears the builders abandoned, thus establishing a new trend in design. Nineteenth-century restoration retained the fifteenth-century roof and pulpit. The roof has 350 panels carved in oak, each with its own individual carved boss. Every design is different and the rich variations in the tone of the wood enhance the fine craftsmanship. There are few more impressive roofs in Britain. While the woodworkers were busy in the roof it is likely that the masons were occupied with the task of creating the pulpit. This marvellous piece of work was cut from a single stone and set on a post. It can be reached only by climbing steps cut through a stone pier. Very few such examples remain in England today and this is one of the finest.

Staple Fitzpaine: St Peter.

The church nestles in the small hamlet against the backdrop of the hill topped by the remains of Castle Neroche (see chapter 5). The church has one of the finest towers in the county, dating from the fifteenth century, with pierced battlements and comical gargoyles. The south doorway is Norman and unusual in its rich decoration. The small wooden screen came from the neighbouring church at Bickenhall; all that is left of its own screen is the beautiful chair at the priest's desk.

Stawley: St Michael.

This delightful little church dates from the eleventh and thirteenth centuries and is unusual in having had no nineteenth-century alterations. Inside there are high pews and an elevated pulpit with a domed canopy and a long box pew which encloses the choir. The font is some seven hundred years old, and above the doorway to the tower is an interesting frieze of twelve panels requesting prayers for two long-departed souls.

Stogursey: St Andrew.

The west doorway and the deep tub font here are Norman, as are the arches supporting the wide central tower. Two smaller arches were added when the side chapels were built in the thirteenth century. The font merits close examination, with four old faces peering out between bands of ornamentation. The nave was rebuilt in the fifteenth century and from a century later there are records dating the carving of the splendid bench ends. These depict a man climbing a tree, a great fish and birds hiding in a mass of foliage. On one of the columns in the chapel is an iron ring which has been the cause of much local debate. It is believed to have been used to secure strangers who took sanctuary in the church so that they should not escape and bring misfortune to the village. They were eventually released to walk, 'bareheaded and barefooted' down the king's highway to the nearest port. On no ship was ready to take them away, they had to walk waist-deep into the sea each day, to show their willingness to leave the country!

Taunton: St James.

The church is situated just outside the medieval earth-bank defences of the town, near the site of the medieval priory, and is now a familiar landmark to spectators at the adjoining county cricket ground. St James's is the smaller of the pair of towers that dominate Taunton's skyline, and the tower may indeed have served as a pattern for St Mary's and other Quantock churches in a nineteenth-century rebuilding of an earlier fifteenth-century tower. The church is largely Perpendicular in style, having a remarkably lofty chancel. Much of the original fabric can be seen, notably the very fine fifteenth-century octagonal font bowl and a pulpit dated 1633.

Taunton: St Mary Magdalene.

The magnificent tower of St Mary Magdalene can best be viewed from the High Street, looking down Hammet Street which frames the west end of the church. The tower, 163 feet (49.7 metres) high, is fretted with delicate lace-like tracery. The original tower was built in about 1500 when Taunton was revelling in the prosperity of the woollen industry. It was completely rebuilt in the middle of the nineteenth century but the Victorian restorers appear to have copied the original perfectly. The body of the church is small compared with the tower though it is wide, with unusual double aisles on each side.

Trull: All Saints.

Despite its proximity to Taunton, Trull has retained the character of a village, enhanced

Wells Cathedral: the west front.

by the delightful village church. The interior is of especial interest, with a wealth of fifteenth-century carving. The bench ends depict scenes from a religious procession and there are fine ancient screens across the chancel and side chapels. The wooden pulpit is very rare in its design, with five canopied niches containing carved statues.

Wedmore: St Mary.
Most of this church dates from the twelfth century and it is an early example of the cruciform design. The most magnificent feature is the south doorway, which was very probably designed and carved by the masons who worked on Wells Cathedral. There are two murals of St Christopher, one painted above the other, and beautifully sculptured bench ends. Some of these are modern, but equally fine and interesting in that they depict, symbolically, the rural crafts and industries associated with the area: peat, willows, strawberries and cheese.

Wellington: St John the Baptist.
This handsome church is the first major building to be seen in the town when approaching from the east. It was rebuilt in the fifteenth century and restored in the nineteenth. Among numerous interesting features are the ornamental Early English window at the east end, a fourteenth-century statue of a priest and a carved crucifix with lilies forming part of the window in the south chapel. There is also the canopied tomb of Sir John Popham, who was Lord Chief Justice at

the trials of Guy Fawkes and Sir Walter Raleigh.

Wells: Cathedral Church of St Andrew.
No visitor to Somerset should fail to visit Wells Cathedral. Since the appeal to preserve the amazing carvings on the west front (floodlit at night), it has become a national attraction and a national concern. First and foremost it is a beautiful church. From a distance its towers rise above the rooftops and chimneys of the surrounding town as other cathedrals must have done before modern high-rise blocks obliterated their silhouettes. In Wells the skyline has scarcely altered over eight hundred years.

Approach the Cathedral from the High Street and Market Place through Penniless Porch and out on to the expansive green. Surrounding the green are some beautiful medieval houses, many refaced in the eighteenth and nineteenth centuries. Pass the west front, with its rich adornment of restored carvings, and to your right you will find the famous clock with mechanical figures which strike the bells to sound the quarters. Pass under the enclosed footbridge which connects the Vicars' Close with the Cathedral — built to avoid too much contact with laymen (and women) when going to and fro — and turn left into the Close, the oldest inhabited complete street in Europe. Only one of the cottages has retained its minute medieval windows and its high-walled patch of garden. The tiny chapel which closes the north end of the street was built in about 1470; it includes an intricately

25

worked screen and some interesting *repoussé* panels in late nineteenth-century Arts and Crafts style by Heywood Sumner.

The dominating and unusual features of the nave of the Cathedral are the massive inverted arches. There are four of them, each supporting the central tower, but they were not part of the original structure. The tower was constructed in the early fourteenth century, and soon after it was built it had to be reinforced. With great ingenuity, these vast arches were fitted in to prop it all up.

In the north transept the interior face of the famous clock of 1390 can be seen, complete with jousting knights which knock one another down as they rotate the hours. From here a staircase, worn uneven by centuries of tramping feet, rises to the chapter house, probably the best example of rib vaulting in Britain. Look out for the humorous carvings on the capitals of some of the pillars: one series tells the story of two thieves caught stealing apples from an orchard; another shows a man pulling a thorn from his foot.

Wells: St Cuthbert.

This ancient parish church is the largest as well as one of the most interesting in Somerset. There has been a church on the site since Saxon times and adjoining the present site is a small mound which probably served as a burial ground. Nothing now remains of the first church, nor indeed of the Norman building that replaced it, save a much mutilated piscina. It was in the thirteenth century, when the style of Early English architecture was at its best, that the foundations were laid around which the present building has grown. Some parts still date from this time, notably the piers and arches of the nave arcade, but during the fifteenth century it was largely rebuilt as part of a massive restoration programme and it is the features left by the masons of that time that created the appearance of the church seen today.

It is characteristically Perpendicular in style. The nave was heightened and extended by one bay at the west end and the magnificent tower was built. The general plan of the church conforms to the customary cruciform plan except that the transepts extend considerably more to the west than is usual in most medieval churches, thereby creating, with the aisles, a number of subsidiary chapels. The nave was later heightened again by the addition of the clerestory and the present low-pitched roof was installed. It is a fine example of sixteenth-century workmanship, lavishly decorated with angels, rosettes and shields.

West Monkton: St Augustine.

The village was named after the monks of Glastonbury and one of their abbots rebuilt the leper's hospital here, which later became almshouses. Externally the lofty tower, bereft of all ornamentation, somehow defies the splendour of the interior of this fifteenth-century church. There is some fine carving and a superb wagon roof. The chancel arch is all that remains of an earlier church on the site dating from the thirteenth century. There is a delightful inscription commemorating the demise of the village doctor, William Kinglake:

'Contention's doubtfull
Where two champions bee;
Thou hast conquered Death,
Now Death hath conquered thee.'

Wiveliscombe: St Andrew.

Although the church itself is relatively recent, built from 1827-9, the most notable feature is the large vaulted undercroft which gives access to extensive catacombs. During the Second World War many of Britain's finest works of art were stored here to protect them from possible bomb damage. Inside the church is a plaque listing the treasures that came.

Barford Park.

7
Historic houses and gardens

Barford Park, Enmore, near Bridgwater. Telephone: 027867 269.

Originally built as a farmhouse, the grand Queen Anne front of two storeys was created in 1710; forty years later a top storey was added to accommodate servants' bedrooms, and the curved wings with the blind arcading and pavilions were built with classical detail in moulded brick. Owned by the Everard family of Otterhampton from the early nineteenth century until 1956, the building and grounds were in a very bad state of repair requiring much restoration by the present owners, Mr and Mrs Michael Stancomb.

Barford and its surrounding park and gardens form a miniature country estate providing an excellent example, on a small scale, of typical Georgian landscaping, looking out over a ha-ha to a well timbered park. The subtle change from farmland to park is scarcely noticeable. There is a fine pond teeming with goldfish, a terrace, lawns and a wonderful water and woodland garden where primulas, gunnera, azaleas and rhododendrons are planted to create a delightful effect of natural wilderness.

Barrington Court, near Ilminster TA19 0NQ. Telephone: 0460 41480. National Trust.

The house was built by Lord Daubeney in 1514, soon after he was married. The walls of warm Ham stone are covered with lichen and each elevation is decorated with fancy twisted finials and triangular gables. The ground plan is E-shaped and from the south almost perfectly symmetrical. The position of the house is superb, surrounded by flat meadows skirted by gentle wooded hills.

Although the exterior has been little altered, the house was restored by Colonel A. Lyle (of Tate and Lyle), who lived here in the 1920s. He also created the gardens with advice from Gertrude Jekyll. Walled iris, rose and lily gardens are linked by attractive brick paths, and a long herbaceous border leads to the productive kitchen garden which operates a pick-your-own scheme in the summer. The house is now leased as a showroom for antique and reproduction furniture. Away from the house and through avenues of trees are some interesting farm buildings and seventeenth-century stables around a courtyard. The village of Barrington, nearby, is delightful and the church has an unusual central eight-sided tower.

Bishop's Palace, Wells. Telephone: 0749 78691.

The magical moated site is bordered on the west by the great cathedral church and cloister and on the east by open fields; visitors enter from an arch off the Market Place, the Bishop's Eye, to a green shaded by mature trees. Beside the drawbridge the swans are trained to ring a bell when they are hungry; the ducks rely on kindly children armed with bags of stale bread. Through a second archway are the grounds and palace, the residence of the Bishops of Bath and Wells since the thirteenth century.

Despite the moat and castellated walls this was never a defensive castle, except perhaps to protect the Bishop from the motley goings-on in the town; the moat and walls were status symbols recognising the Bishop as lord of a great estate. The oldest surviving building is the thirteenth-century hall built by Bishop Jocelin, still roofed and still in use, with an impressive undercroft.

The Jubilee Arboretum was planted to commemorate the Silver Jubilee of the Queen. Further round towards the back of the palace are the 'wells', or rather St Andrew's Well, a large pool fed by subterranean streams from the Mendip Hills, from which the town takes its name.

Brympton d'Evercy, near Yeovil. Telephone: 0935 862528.

This Elizabethan country house, in a picturesque valley isolated from the bustle of Yeovil, is built of rich yellow local Ham stone. The buildings, including the house, Priest House, stables and church, create a picture of rural perfection. The present owner, Charles Clive-Ponsonby-Fane, is dedicated to preserving the house and estate for future generations. It has been in his family since 1731. The most notable feature of the interior is the longest straight staircase in England. The adjoining Priest House, with a first-floor hall, was built in the fifteenth century and is now a country life museum and distillery with a cider still from Calvados (see chapter 8).

On the sheltered south-facing bank on one side of the house is a vineyard, and the wine produced from it can be purchased from the shop.

The 10 acre (4 ha) grounds include daisy, pot-pourri, herbaceous and shrub beds with extensive lawns and have been the subject of much hard restoration work.

Clapton Court Gardens, Crewkerne TA18 8PT. Telephone: 0460 73220 or 72200.

This is one of the most beautiful gardens in the West Country, with a fine collection of rare and unusual plants, shrubs and trees of botanical interest, set in formal and woodland settings extending to 10 acres (4 ha). There is always an outstanding display of spring bulbs, and in the autumn the colours are magnificent. There is a plant centre where one can buy high-quality, more unusual plants; fuchsias and pelargoniums are a speciality.

Coleridge Cottage, 35 Lime Street, Nether Stowey, Bridgwater TA5 1NQ. National Trust.

Samuel Taylor Coleridge lived here from 1797 to 1800, and in that short time he wrote almost all his greatest poems, including 'The Ancient Mariner' and 'Christabel'. His inspiration was no doubt fired by William and Dorothy Wordsworth, who lived for a while, in grander style, at Alfoxton House (now a hotel) at Holford, not far away. They met frequently and walked the beautiful Quantock Hills. The cottage, tiny and thatched, became the Coleridge Cottage Inn until public effort rescued it for the National Trust. The parlour and reading room only are open.

Combe Sydenham, Monksilver, near Taunton. Telephone: 0984 56284.

The present house was erected on medieval foundations by Sir George Sydenham in 1580. One wing and three of the four original towers were probably demolished during the Civil War and there was partial rebuilding after the Restoration in 1660. The place is being revived by its current owners, the Theed family, who are determined to restore the buildings and grounds to their former magnificence.

Legend records that in the sixteenth century the heiress, Elizabeth Sydenham, was courted by Sir Francis Drake after the death of his first wife. He was not generally approved of by her family, but in spite of this he managed to secure a promise from Elizabeth that she would wait for his return from sea. After many months, if not years of waiting, not knowing if her former fiancé was alive or dead, Elizabeth became betrothed to another. On the wedding day, as the bridal party was about to enter the church (it is thought to have been Stogumber), there was a sudden blinding flash and a great cannonball hurtled through the sky to fall between the bride and groom. The portent was unmistakable, and Elizabeth refused to go through with the ceremony. Drake arrived in Plymouth shortly afterwards and hurried to Combe Sydenham, where he finally married Elizabeth in 1585. The great black ball can be seen today in the hall of the house. It weighs over 100 pounds (45 kg) and is thought to be a meteorite.

In addition to the house there are formal gardens, sixteenth-century fish ponds which have been restored and stocked with trout, and a leat through the 'Secret Valley' to the mill and deserted hamlet of Goodley (left to decay after the Black Death). Walks lead through wooded coombs to the High Viewpoint (1000 feet; 304 metres) with panoramic views across the Quantocks as far as the Welsh

Barrington Court: the head of the sundial.   *Combe Sydenham.*

coast, taking in the island of Steep Holme in the Bristol Channel and sweeping across Exmoor and the Blackdown Hills.

Cricket St Thomas, Chard TA20 2DD. Telephone: 046030 755.

Situated on the A30 between Chard and Crewkerne, Cricket House, made known to many as 'Grantleigh Manor' in the television series *To the Manor Born,* is the hub of a working estate and wildlife and leisure park extending to some 1000 acres (400 ha), owned and run by the Taylor family.

The name 'Cricket' is derived from the Anglo-Saxon word *cruc* meaning a hill or ridge and the estate is described in the Domesday Book of 1087. The house, of honey-coloured stone, was designed by John Soane in the 1780s for Rear Admiral Alexander Hood and presents an interesting and attractive example of his work. It replaced an earlier manor house that was burnt down in the eighteenth century. The gracious yet informal gardens extend to 16 acres (6.5 ha) and contain hundreds of rare shrubs and magnificent trees. See chapter 9 for the wildlife park.

East Lambrook Manor, East Lambrook, near Martock, South Petherton. Telephone: 0460 40328.

Here a fifteenth-century house built of local

Ham stone stands within the garden created by one of the best loved gardeners of the twentieth century, Margery Fish. It is justifiably registered as a Grade 1 garden and is an example of the very best in the traditional English cottage style. Plants propagated from the garden can be bought in the Margery Fish Nursery.

Fyne Court, Broomfield, Bridgwater TA5 2EQ. National Trust.

Fyne Court is now the Visitor Centre of the Somerset Trust for Nature Conservation. The house was built in 1634 but was burnt out in 1898, and only the Andrew Crosse Hall and the outbuildings survive today. For most of its history the house was in the hands of the Crosse and Hamilton families. Andrew Crosse gained some notoriety in the early nineteenth century for his experiments into the use of electrical energy and his startling statements about its future use, which time has proved correct.

The Trust has its offices and workshops in the old coach house and there is also a small shop. The interpretation centre of the natural history of the area is well worth visiting before setting off on a choice of trails leading through picturesque woodland surrounding a lush valley. Look out for badger sets and kingfishers on the lake.

29

Gaulden Manor.

Gaulden Manor, Tolland, near Taunton. Telephone: 09847 213.

Smaller than most of the other houses open to the public in Somerset, Gaulden Manor is well worth seeing. It is a manor house of great charm dating from the twelfth century and was the home of two famous families, the Turbervilles of Bere Regis, immortalised by Thomas Hardy in *Tess of the D'Urbervilles*, and the Woolcotts. Henry Woolcott emigrated to America from Gaulden in 1628 to found one of the oldest families in the United States.

The seventeenth-century hall has an impressive low plaster ceiling with all manner of roundels and garlands. Notice the crude figures in the plasterwork over the fireplace. The gardens are well cared for, with a specialist herb garden and a bog garden, and visitors return annually to enjoy the peace and quiet of this secluded place. A visit in the spring to see the primulas is well worthwhile.

Hadspen Garden and Nursery, Laundry Cottage, Hadspen House, Castle Cary BA7 7NG. Telephone: 0963 50939.

The eighteenth-century house is not open to the public but the restored Edwardian garden of 8 acres (3.2 ha) is. It is set on a sheltered south-facing slope and has a colourist walled garden and romantic woodland walk. Both garden and nursery feature choice herbaceous plants and old-fashioned and modern roses.

Halsway Manor, Crowcombe. Telephone: 09848 274.

Halsway Manor is run by the Halsway Manor Society as a residential folk centre where enthusiasts from all over Britain can meet to share their pleasure in folk dancing and music. Most visitors stay for a weekend or week, but day visitors are also welcomed to enjoy the house and gardens.

The history of the house spans nine centuries; it was mentioned in the Domesday Book as 'Halsweie', possibly derived from Hazel Way — a prehistoric track over the Quantocks. The oldest surviving part of the house is the library, dating from the sixteenth century; the fine panelling, by a local craftsman, was not fitted until the nineteenth century.

Hatch Court, Hatch Beauchamp, Taunton TA3 6AA. Telephone: 0823 480208.

This fine Bath stone mansion, built in the Palladian style and set in a deer park, was designed by Thomas Prowse of Axbridge in 1755. The main building is rectangular with a small tower at each corner. In about 1800 a curving orangery was added to the west side and in order to maintain the symmetry a curved screen was erected on the east side. One of the features of the building is the arcaded loggia in the centre of the main facade. Inside, a splendid stone staircase fills the middle of the house and the drawing room has a fine plasterwork ceiling. There is also the China Room, probably the only one of this kind in England, and a small Canadian regimental museum.

Hestercombe House, Cheddon Fitzpaine, Taunton TA2 8LQ. Telephone: 0823 337222. Somerset County Council (Fire Brigade Headquarters).

Until about 1900 the house was surrounded by meadows and parkland. Sir Edwin Lutyens was then commissioned to lay down formal gardens and, with Gertrude Jekyll, built the existing intricate scheme, reminiscent of Elizabethan design, between 1904 and 1910. Lutyens designed the Orangery on the east side of the garden overlooking the sweeping lawns. Unfortunately the gardens fell into decline and were saved only by the intervention of the Fire Brigade which first occupied the house and grounds in 1953. Since the 1970s the gardens have been lovingly restored and visitors can once again enjoy walking the raised pathways with extensive views over the vale of Taunton, or relish the peace and tranquillity of the sunken formal garden.

Lytes Cary Manor, Charlton Mackrell, Somerton TA11 7HU. National Trust.

This picturesque small Somerset manor house was the home for five hundred years of the Lyte family. Here was the garden upon which Sir Henry Lyte based his *Niewe Herball,* published in 1578, the most important horticultural work of that time. The present beautiful garden was laid out in Elizabethan style by Sir Walter Jenner early in the twentieth century.

The buildings once stood on four sides of the courtyard. Now, only the Great Hall, chapel and one part of the dwelling house survive.

The orangery at Hestercombe House.

The hall is magnificent, with an impressive roof of moulded collar beams and cusped windbraces. The walls are panelled and the room is furnished with seventeenth-century oak benches, chairs and tables. It is easy to imagine a grand banquet in such a setting, with colourfully dressed entertainers performing on the balcony overlooking the feast.

Maunsel House, North Newton, near Bridgwater. Telephone: 0278 663413.

Most of the house dates from 1420 when the Great Hall was built, although fragments of earlier buildings are said to pre-date the Norman conquest. In 1086 the manor was named 'Maunsel' — from the French meaning 'a sleeve of land' — and it was granted to Count Eustace of Boulogne, kinsman of William the Conqueror. At the time of Henry II, William de Erleigh granted Maunsel to Philip Arbalistarius as a dowry to his daughter Mabel on payment of two pigs every Whitsuntide at his Court of Durston. His son Philip married the daughter of Sir Hugh D'Auderville and assumed the surname of Maunsel. From the Maunsel family the estate eventually passed to the Bacon family of Norfolk and then to the Slades.

Midelney Manor, Drayton, near Langport TA10 0NU.

Originally an island manor of the Abbots of Muchelney and home of the Trevilian family since the sixteenth century, it has a fine walled garden, seventeenth-century falcon mews and heronry.

Milton Lodge Gardens, Wells. Telephone: 0747 72168.

From the glorious tumbling terrace of trim

Montacute House: one of the gazebos.

lawns and square yew hedges on the steep south-facing scarp of the Mendip Hills there are superb views over the cathedral city of Wells and the Vale of Avalon beyond. There are colourful borders of mixed shrubs including old-fashioned rose beds and climbers. Across the Old Bristol Road is the 7 acre (2.8 ha) arboretum of towering specimen trees.

The garden was created in 1909 by the present owner's grandfather, but it has been substantially replanted since the early 1960s.

Montacute House, Montacute, Yeovil TA15 6XP. Telephone: 0935 823289. National Trust.

This magnificent mansion was begun in 1588, the year of the Armada, for Sir Edward Phelips, Speaker of the House of Commons, by William Arnold, who also did much work on Dunster Castle. The formal gardens and lush countryside provide a perfect setting for the mellow Ham stone house. Visitors enter the house from the east side, where the H-shaped plan is clearly visible. In front, the gardens end in a balustrade with summer-houses at each corner which frame the parkland beyond.

It is superbly furnished with sixteenth- and seventeenth-century paintings, furniture and tapestries and eighteenth-century ceramics. Carefully concealed behind panelled doors in one of the bedrooms is a neat bathroom complete with a cast iron bath, an Edwardian innovation which still required bevies of domestic servants to carry down the waste. In the main hall there is an interesting plaster frieze depicting 'skimmetty riding' (to ride skimmetty was the fate of a man who was hen-pecked). In this panel the husband is shown being beaten over the head by his wife with a shoe and then being paraded around the village on a pole. One wonders why such a decoration was chosen for one of the principal rooms in the house.

The long gallery, reputed to be the longest in England (189 feet; 58 metres), and adjoining rooms have been used to house an exhibition of sixteenth- and seventeenth-century portraits on loan from the National Portrait Gallery. The National Trust shop is in the old laundry next to the car park. The formal gardens, gazebos, orangery and archery lawns are a delight. The park was re-landscaped in the nineteenth century and provides a worthy setting for the house.

Poundisford Park, Pitminster, near Taunton TA3 7AF. Telephone: 082342 244.

Poundisford Park, beautifully situated in the former deer park of Taunton Castle, is a charming example of Tudor country architecture, begun in 1546, and perfectly preserved with very little alteration. The entrance leads into a screens passage which runs across the house and gives access to the great hall, a fine room with an elaborate sixteenth-century plaster ceiling, one of many in the house. There is a small display of eighteenth- and nineteenth-century costumes in one of the bedrooms. Visitors are free to wander in the large, simple garden, typical of the Tudor style and including an unusual seventeenth-century brick summerhouse.

Simonsbath House, Simonsbath, Exmoor TA24 7SH. Telephone: 064383 259.

Simonsbath House was built by James Boevey, the first owner of Exmoor, shortly after he took over the freehold in 1652. The site he chose marked the junction of all the moorland tracks, almost in the centre of the wilderness, on high land above the river Barle. On the death of Boevey's widow the house passed into the hands of a disreputable character who let it go to rack and ruin, and ended up burning most of the interior timberwork as firewood whilst barricaded inside to escape arrest. The enormous oak front door, still bearing axe marks, remains to this day. After his tenancy, the house passed through the hands of numerous foresters, and at one time became an inn, until about 1827 when the house was taken over by John Knight (see chapter 1). He began to build a new house above the old one and planned to demolish the latter, but owing to lack of funds his dreams were never realised and the shell of his new house stood unfinished until it was demolished about 1900. Subsequently, the house became a base for hunting parties and social gatherings and was expanded and improved, largely by the Fortescue family in the 1920s. They were responsible for the fine panelling and fireplaces and also built one of the first squash courts in England in 1929. The house is now run as a country house hotel, but visitors are welcome to look around whilst enjoying coffee or a cream tea.

Somerset College of Agriculture and Horticulture, Cannington, near Bridgwater. Somerset County Council.

Beautiful old sandstone-walled gardens protect a range of plants including many less hardy species — ceanothus, fremontias, wistarias. The ten large greenhouses contain an exceptional array of ornamental plants as well as banana, orange, sugarcane, tea, papaya and passion fruit. This must be one of the largest collections of ornamental plants in south-west England, planted for landscape effect and arranged for ease of identification. There are experimental gardens with lawn grass collections and trials and beautiful views towards the Quantocks. It is open occasionally.

Tintinhull House Garden, Tintinhull, near Yeovil BA22 8PZ. National Trust.

The east front of the house, with mullioned windows and arched doorways, is all that remains of the late sixteenth-century farmhouse which stood on this site. The rest of the house which can be seen today dates from the eighteenth century. It is not open to the public. The garden was laid out initially by Dr Price, a distinguished botanist, between 1898 and 1924. Later improvements added a formal garden with rectangular pool, loggia and yew hedges. Each section of the garden is a delight throughout the year as the borders contain a mixture of bulbs, grasses, foliage plants and flowering shrubs, all overlooked by an ancient cedar tree.

West Somerset Museum, Allerford.

8
Museums

ALLERFORD
West Somerset Museum, The Old School, Allerford.

Set in the old village school the museum splendidly recreates the atmosphere of a Victorian schoolroom with the teacher's desk overlooking rows of children's desks, carved and ink-stained, with copy books and toys. There is also a rural collection with a Victorian cottage kitchen, laundry and dairy and exhibitions of local crafts. Demonstrations of spinning and woodcarving take place here during the summer months, as well as conducted walking tours of the village and neighbourhood. Light refreshments are available.

AXBRIDGE
Axbridge Museum: King John's Hunting Lodge, The Square, Axbridge. Telephone: 0934 732012. National Trust and Sedgemoor District Council.

This small three-storey timber-framed building faces the square in the centre of Axbridge. It is a late medieval merchant's house, which originally had shops on the ground floor, with heavy wooden boards covering the 'windows' which were lowered to form the counters.

No one knows why the building is known as

King John's Hunting Lodge, although King John did own the Cheddar and Axbridge estate as part of his Royal Forest of Mendip, he loved hunting and often visited the area: he was also responsible for granting Axbridge its first royal charter. This building in the centre of the town appeared older than the others and had a king's head carved on the outside, so this, it was deduced, must have been his hunting lodge. The true royal hunting lodge, a fine country palace, had been totally lost and forgotten. It was rediscovered only in 1960, not at Axbridge, but in Cheddar. But the name stuck to the house in Axbridge, although it was built about three hundred years after King John and the carving on the building is later still, possibly part of an inn sign erected when the house was the King's Head alehouse in the seventeenth and eighteenth centuries.

The museum contains a variety of local archaeological finds and geological specimens from some of the nearby caves. One fascinating skeleton is that of a young man found in a post-Roman cemetery at Banwell. The skeleton bears no evidence of the reason for his death, but it does show that he suffered from a mild form of spina bifida. Notice the 'nail'; it was made by Thomas Pennington in

34

1627 and probably stood outside the entrance of the old Guildhall on the north side of the Market Place. Commercial transactions were concluded across it, hence the saying 'to pay on the nail'.

BRIDGWATER
Admiral Blake Museum, Blake Street, Bridgwater. Telephone: 0278 456127. Sedgemoor District Council.

The celebrated Admiral Blake was born in this house in 1598. He was the Member of Parliament for Bridgwater in 1640 and distinguished himself in the Civil War in an heroic defence of Taunton. He then embarked upon an outstanding naval career and was appointed one of the 'Generals at Sea'. His statue, on the Cornhill in the centre of Bridgwater, was unveiled in 1900. The museum contains a variety of objects of local interest, archaeological specimens, relics of the battle of Sedgemoor, watercolours and photographs of the town. Of particular interest is the exhibition on brick and tile making, recalling the prosperity of the town in the nineteenth century when most of the population was employed in the industry. The Alford Room contains mementoes of grander style: some lovely eighteenth- and nineteenth-century family portraits and personalia from three local families, including snuffboxes and canes.

BRYMPTON D'EVERCY
Brympton Museum, Brympton d'Evercy, near Yeovil. Telephone: 0935 862528.

Right beside the great house, this smaller but equally delightful building houses an interesting collection of rural artefacts, some associated with the estate. The exhibition includes a particularly good array of early cidermaking equipment, huge wooden beamed presses, apple-crushing mills and barrels exuding the aroma of rich brews from seasons past.

CASTLE CARY
Castle Cary Museum, The Market Place, Castle Cary BA7 7AA. Telephone: 0963 50277.

This small museum of objects from the immediate locality includes archaeological finds, agricultural and craft tools and a collection of Victorian domestic items illustrating cottage and farmhouse life. There are also some items from local industries.

CHARD
Chard and District Museum, Godworthy House, High Street, Chard TA20 1QL. Telephone: 0460 202500.

Displayed in a modernised seventeenth-century house with a thatched roof and mullioned windows, the collections illustrate

aspects of the history of Chard and the surrounding area. One extraordinary and rather macabre section contains the remnants of the workshop of John Gillingham, a nineteenth-century artificial-limb maker. It includes his forge and photographs of some of the disabled he equipped with cumbersome limbs and appliances. In the back room is a good example of a wooden horse gear from a nearby farm. It was used to power a cider mill and was restored and installed by volunteers. Aviation enthusiasts will find much interest in the collections associated with John Stringfellow, the inventor of the first power-driven aircraft. A complete double-bellows blacksmith's forge and a local carpenter's workshop have been re-created in one of the outbuildings. Upstairs is a costume gallery.

Hornsbury Mill, Eleighwater, near Chard TA20 3AQ. Telephone: 04606 3317.

The nineteenth-century watermill houses a rural bygones museum. The mill, built in the 1830s, worked commercially until about 1942. All the machinery is still intact and the guide leaflet claims that 'it could be used to grind corn at any time'. One feature is the miller's lavatory — complete with mounting block! The waterwheel, 18 feet (5.5 metres) in diameter and six feet (1.8 metres) wide, is a good example of an overshot wheel. It was made by Bodley Brothers of Exeter and installed by Joseph Hawker, millwright, of Chard.

Among the historic graffiti found by the owners when clearing the mill was the following verse:

'God bless our wives, they fill our hives
With little bees and honey.
They soothe life's shocks,
They mend our socks
But don't they spend the money.'

The bygones were collected by Mr Austin Wookey of East Harptree and make up a fascinating and amusing exhibition.

EVERCREECH
Cutterne Mill, Southwood, near Evercreech, Shepton Mallet BA4 6LY. Telephone: 0749 830331.

Cutterne Mill, a privately owned watermill, was built in 1628. The massive waterwheel you can see today was installed in 1862 and was last used in the 1930s. The folk museum has a comprehensive display of the history of Cutterne Mill, ranging from its earliest recording in the Domesday survey until the present day, with photographs of its more recent inhabitants from 1850 onwards. Victorian and Edwardian clothing is on show together with various everyday items, including some beautiful magic lantern slides. On the ground floor there is a fascinating documentation of corn milling through the ages. Outside there are farm animals and a pets' corner, a nature trail, a picnic area and a shop which stocks local craft products.

FROME
Frome Museum, 1 North Parade, Frome. Enquiries to the Museum Administrator, telephone: 0373 62371.

The museum is run as a charity on a volunteer basis and has accumulated a fine display of objects relating to local geology, archaeology, industrial archaeology and social history. Items of special interest include the best preserved iron age quern in Britain, a Victorian fire engine, a costume collection, including some from the Horner family (of Little Jack Horner) and a reconstruction of a local chemist's shop which had been established in Frome for more than a century. There are also regular temporary exhibitions. The museum shop sells books on local history and other items of local interest.

GLASTONBURY
Glastonbury Lake Village Museum, The Tribunal, High Street, Glastonbury. English Heritage.

It is easy to miss this small museum halfway up the High Street just below St John's church. The Tribunal, or Court House, where cases were tried under the authority of the Abbot of Glastonbury, is a fine example of fifteenth-century architecture and is an interesting monument in itself. The heavy black door through which you enter is surmounted by a Tudor rose and a coat of arms in stone. The museum houses the finds from the iron age lake villages at Meare and Glastonbury which were excavated by a local medical practitioner, Arthur Bulleid, and St George Grey, the curator of Taunton Castle between 1892 and 1933. The peculiar properties of peat soil helped to preserve even wooden artefacts and seeds. The two-thousand-year-old saw and sickle on display here were used on one occasion as models for an iron-age village reconstruction experiment on television. More recent relics of Glastonbury's history are also shown, with medieval tiles from the Abbey and Jack Stag, a rude stone carving that formerly adorned the market cross.

Somerset Rural Life Museum, Abbey Farm, Chilkwell Street, Glastonbury BA6 8DB. Telephone: 0458 32903. Somerset County Council.

The magnificent fourteenth-century Abbey Barn is the centrepiece of the Somerset Rural Life Museum which houses a magnificent display of old carts and farm machinery, gleaned from the surrounding countryside. The farm buildings around the courtyard have been sympathetically restored and now house interesting collections depicting local activities like willow growing, basketmaking, mud-horse fishing, peat digging and cidermaking. In the Abbey Farmhouse the social and domestic life of Victorian Somerset is depicted through the life story of John Hodges, a Victorian farm labourer who lived in the nearby village of Butleigh. The story of his life is told in vivid and simple style, using museum objects and illustrations.

The farmhouse kitchen has been reconstructed with a comprehensive display of culinary implements and the cellar represents a traditional farmhouse Cheddar cheese room, complete with all the equipment used in the nineteenth century. One section of the museum contains specimens of local folklore: it includes a model of the famous Minehead hobby horse, a stone amulet and a bottle containing a crucifix and tools of the Passion. There are also two shrivelled hearts said to have been used to ward off evil spirits by nailing them in a chimney.

Other attractions include a variety of events and entertainments during the summer season, especially those with a local flavour. You can watch buttermaking using traditional churns, or see cidermaking in the autumn, and enjoy traditional craft demonstrations and morris dancing displays.

PORLOCK
Porlock Museum, Doverhay Manor, Porlock. Telephone: 0643 862357.

This tiny museum, which shares its premises with the Tourist Information Office, aims to illustrate Porlock's past. For the most part the exhibits are old photographs and paintings of the village, with a small display of press cuttings, and tools associated with local trades.

SPARKFORD
Sparkford Motor Museum, Sparkford, near Yeovil BA22 7LH. Telephone: 0963 40804.

In 1985 John Haynes of the Haynes Publishing Group established the museum with his fine collection of vintage and veteran cars and motorcycles. Vehicles in the museum range from a 1905 Daimler detachable-top limousine to an AC Cobra, the world's fastest production sports car. The display area is surrounded by an interesting collection of motor memorabilia. Every car in the museum is maintained in full working order and all are driven at least once every six months. The museum is dedicated to restore, retain and preserve motoring and motorcycling items of historical and cultural interest, and exhibits are in as near to pristine condition as the day they were manufactured.

Somerset Rural Life Museum, Abbey Farm, Glastonbury.

STREET

The Shoe Museum, High Street, Street. Telephone: 0458 43131.

The museum is in the oldest part of the C. and J. Clark factory in the High Street. There are nineteenth-century documents and photographs illustrating the early history of the Clark family and the production of shoes and other leather goods, initially on an outwork basis and later in the factory. Some of the earliest machines produced rugs, mops and chamois leathers from local sheepskins before shoemaking began in earnest in the 1840s. From that time the story is well documented, with many old tools on display and a comprehensive array of shoes dating from Roman times until 1950 — a fascinating microcosm of fashion.

TAUNTON

Somerset County Museum, Taunton Castle, Taunton. Telephone: 0823 55504. Somerset County Council and Somerset Archaeological and Natural History Society.

Pass under the portcullis in the south gate and enter the courtyard or inner bailey of Taunton Castle. The museum is housed in the Great Hall and adjoining galleries. There was probably a Saxon fortress on or near this site in the ninth or tenth century. Nothing of that remains, but on the right-hand side of the courtyard note the twelfth-century foundations of the old castle keep.

In the present Great Hall, with its modern displays, it is hard to imagine the scene there in 1685 when Judge Jeffreys in two days tried 514 supporters of the Duke of Monmouth, sentencing 146 of them to death, after the battle of Sedgemoor. The museum has a particularly important collection of local archaeological finds and these have been displayed in the Wyndham Gallery. The exhibition tells the story of man's early struggle for existence in the forests and marshes of the county. The showpiece of the collection is the famous Low Ham mosaic, a masterpiece of Roman craftsmanship. The story ends with examples of medieval woodcarving and slip-glazed pottery from Donyatt, near Chard.

Other displays of importance include a gallery devoted to the history of the Somerset Light Infantry, local industrial bygones, including a working beam engine in the entrance hall, a natural history gallery and a doll section. The Great Hall has become a museum of arts and crafts, with an unlikely collection of Chinese pottery, and Somerset products, from silver spoons, clocks and watches to lace and patchwork.

WASHFORD

Somerset and Dorset Railway Museum, Washford, near Minehead. Enquiries to Mike Palmer, telephone: 0278 722207.

This museum at Washford station on the West Somerset Railway is packed with

Watchet: the Market House Museum.

memorabilia from the heyday of the Somerset and Dorset Railway. There are models, photographs, old tickets and a slide collection, and outside there are locomotives, coaches and wagons in various stages of restoration. Try your hand in the working signal box, which operates an on-site signal, and change the shunting points.

WATCHET
The Market House Museum, Market Street, Watchet. Telephone: 0643 7132.

Appropriately situated near the harbour slipway, this small museum is centred on the town's maritime history and harbour activity. It includes exhibits of local finds from prehistoric times to the present day, with photographs, paintings, fossils, Victoriana and the story of the town's Saxon mint. There are also objects from the nineteenth-century ore miners on the Brendon Hills and the old mineral railway. The museum has an audio-visual unit, showing slides with a recorded commentary. 'Watchet 1000', celebrated in 1988, commemorates a Danish raid on the settlement in 988.

WELLINGTON
Wellington Museum, 28 Fore Street, Wellington TA21 8AG. Telephone: 082347 4747.

A small museum illustrating aspects of the town's history, it is housed in the former Squirrel Hotel, a bustling coaching inn in the eighteenth century which continued in use as an hotel until the closure of the Wellington railway station. The museum room has exposed timber beams and two open fireplaces. Temporary exhibitions are mounted regularly. The museum is run entirely by volunteers and is open only during the summer months.

WELLS
Wells Museum, 8 Cathedral Green, Wells BA5 2UE. Telephone: 0749 73477.

Perhaps enjoying the finest setting of any museum in Britain, Wells Museum overlooks the Cathedral Green and the west front. It is delightfully old-fashioned, with a characteristic clutter and sense of discovery. There are important geological and archaeological exhibits, including Roman lead ingots from the mines at Charterhouse and the best finds from the caves at Wookey Hole and Cheddar. Relics of the cathedral include plaster-casts made of some of the west-front sculptures for the Great Exhibition of 1851. It is daunting to come face to face with them and to appreciate the delicacy and craft of the carving.

One room is devoted to a collection of samplers, many worked by children of tender years, with devotional verses carefully created hour after hour.

WILLITON
Orchard Mill, off Bridge Street, Williton. Telephone: 0984 32133.

A good collection of local rural and domestic bygones is exhibited in this seventeenth-century mill on the outskirts of Williton; the mill machinery is not original but it gives a clear understanding of the method of grinding corn using an overshot waterwheel to drive the grindstones. The mill continued in use until its 350th anniversary in 1966, when the last miller, Reg Sutton, retired. It was first opened to the public in 1979.

YEOVIL
Museum of South Somerset, Hendford, Yeovil BA20 1UN. Telephone: 0935 24774.

The museum is housed in the former coach house of Hendford Manor. Although relatively small, the museum is well presented and informative, with some interesting displays. The Stilby Collection of firearms is particularly notable, rivalled only by national museums. There is some fine glassware from the Pinney Collection, a Cromwellian bracket clock, and a display of costumes which is frequently changed to provide continual interest. The upper gallery is devoted to the archaeology of the area, including local prehistoric and Roman remains and a dolphin mosaic from Ilchester Mead. Yeovil's former staple industry is depicted in an interesting exhibition on glove manufacturing through the ages, and there are several old sewing machines on show. Around the walls is an extensive display of photographs of Yeovil past and present.

YEOVILTON
Fleet Air Arm and Concorde Museum, Royal Naval Air Station, Yeovilton BA22 8HT. Telephone: 0935 840565. Royal Navy.

The museum was opened in 1964 by the Duke of Edinburgh. It portrays the historic achievements of the Royal Naval Air Service, and subsequently the Fleet Air Arm, from the early days of kites and airships to the Sea Harriers and helicopters of the present day. Over fifty examples of classic naval aircraft spanning more than eighty years of naval aviation are on show, in addition to hundreds of photographs, models and paintings. Concorde already finds a place here: this is Concorde 002, the first prototype to be built in England. It completed its development flying in 1974 and was ferried from Fairford to Yeovilton by Brian Trubshaw and his original crew on 4th March 1976. The Concorde Hall also contains a mock-up of a Concorde passenger compartment and has displays telling the story of the development of passenger supersonic flight, including two other aircraft used in the test programme.

Flights from the Royal Naval Air Station can be watched from the museum and there is a well stocked souvenir gift shop.

9
Other places to visit

BIRD GARDENS

Ambleside Aviaries and Water Gardens, Lower Weare, near Cheddar. Telephone: 0934 732362.

More than an acre of carefully landscaped pleasure gardens surround the lake at Ambleside; there are many exotic birds including friendly mynahs, macaws and toucans. Children can feed the rabbits, doves and ducks in Pets' Corner.

Tropical Bird Garden, Brean Down. Telephone: 027875 209.

This is a small private collection of birds from all over the world. The garden, in a wooden enclosure, is set at the foot of Brean Down only yards from the sea. Over a hundred different species of birds are shown, including talking mynahs, pheasants and quails, macaws and cockatoos.

Widcombe Bird Gardens, Culmhead, near Taunton. Telephone: 082342 268.

There are beautiful gardens with azaleas and rhododendrons and 20 acres (8 ha) of parkland containing llamas, donkeys, deer, sheep and miniature Shetland ponies as well as a host of birds.

CAVES

Cheddar Caves, Cheddar. Telephone: 0934 742742.

Caving is a dangerous if not a deadly sport, to be undertaken by experts only or under expert supervision; never enter a cave without the permission and authority of the relevant caving club. Dotted about Cheddar are more than four hundred caves or holes, most of them inaccessible, and others barred by a gate or fence. Some of the most spectacular cave systems have been opened commercially for easy public access.

Cox's Cave was discovered in 1837 by George Cox; it contains some superb stalagmite pillars and stalactite curtains. The names of some of these formations conjure up a wonderful picture: Marble Curtain, Peal of Bells, Bunch of Carrots, Lady Chapel, Mermaid and Mummy and Home of the Rainbow.

In 1890 Richard Gough found some of the largest cave chambers in the area, whilst digging with his sons. Gough's Cave now has a tunnel a quarter of a mile (400 metres) long penetrating deep into the rock. It was here that a man broke the world record for surviving alone in 1966; he lived in the boulder chamber for 130 days. In the museum are the remains of a man who lived in the caves in palaeolithic times 10,000 years ago. More

adventurous visitors over twelve years old can don helmet, lamp and boiler suit and go adventure caving.

The energetic can best enjoy the open air scenery of the Cheddar Gorge by climbing Jacob's Ladder, a flight of over three hundred steps up the cliff face, to a tower providing magnificent views of the local hills, the Somerset Moors, the Quantocks, Exmoor and the Bristol Channel. At the top there is the Mendip Appreciation Centre, which explains the countryside around, and it is possible to go orienteering under instruction.

Wookey Hole Caves, Wookey Hole, Wells BA5 1BB. Telephone: 0749 72243. Madame Tussaud's.

The village of Wookey Hole straddles the river Axe just below the point at which the water emerges from the rock. Since the middle ages tourists have visited the village in order to explore the famous caves. It is recorded that in 1709 a party of six visitors was charged 2s 6d to see the caves. They had no guide but were supplied with candles and beer. In 1973 Madame Tussaud's purchased the caves and the adjoining paper mill, and since then they have created an unusual tourist complex comprising caves, papermaking mill, fairground exhibition and waxworks exhibition.

Visitors today purchase a comprehensive ticket which allows access to all the varied attractions. A guide leads parties through the caves, now paved and dramatically lit, pointing out the hook-nosed effigy of the Witch of Wookey, the exploits of cave divers and explorers and the archaeological story of the lives of the cave dwellers who lived here between 250 BC and AD 400. Some of the finds from the caves are displayed at the cave entrance, but the best collection is in the museum in Wells (see chapter 8).

A modern hydro-electric turbine drives the paper-mill machinery but the 12 foot (3.6 metre) overshot waterwheel made in 1980 is a reminder of the original source of power.

In the mill paper is still made by hand and the visitor can see the rags swilling about in troughs, the papermaker filling his meshed tray and the finished sheets hanging up like washing in the drying rooms. It remains one of the few places where it is still possible to purchase fine-quality handmade paper, ideal for watercolour painting or as very special writing paper.

The fairground exhibition consists largely of pieces which belonged originally to Lady Bangor. It includes some outstanding exam-

Ambleside Aviaries and Water Gardens.

ples of woodcarving and painting; an unfinished horse's head carved by Arthur Anderson of Bristol reveals the intricate detail and endless care taken in the preparation of the merry-go-round animals, before they are embellished with the familiar bright colours of the fairground. There are primitive 1930s moon rockets and painted racing cars from mechanical rides and a Marenghi organ. An elaborate display recreates the fun of a 'Penny Pier Arcade', with machines to test your strength or your ingenuity, others to peep into or drive into action, like the stilted mechanical footballers.

The final bizarre attraction is the Madame Tussaud's 'Cabinet of Curiosities', the name given to the travelling waxworks show which toured round Britain for thirty years before the display became established in its Baker Street home in London. Today at Wookey you can see the figures of Madame Tussaud and her family setting up their show in an imaginary Georgian town and have a sneak preview of the main attractions.

CIDERMAKING
Perry's Cider Mills, Dowlish Wake, near Ilminster TA19 0NY. Telephone: 0460 52681.

The traditional cider mills are situated in the heart of the unspoilt village of Dowlish Wake, and the cider is made in a sixteenth-century thatched barn. In autumn, when the local apples have been picked they are brought to the press and crushed. The juice is fermented and allowed to mature naturally in wooden barrels. In addition to the press-house and barrels, there is an interesting new thatched

wagon shed which houses several old wagons and carts and a fine collection of small farm tools. There is also a comprehensive photographic display showing the process of cidermaking, and nostalgic pictures of village life around 1900. In the church is the tomb of John Hanning Speke, who discovered the source of the Nile: Dr David Livingstone attended his funeral here.

Sheppy's Cider, Three Bridges, Bradford-on-Tone, Taunton. Telephone: 0823 461233.

The museum of cidermaking and rural life contains some fascinating local treasures from the days of horse transport and hand labour; the huge wood-screwed cider press is a rare masterpiece. Other buildings contain the modern paraphernalia of cidermaking on a medium scale, which is the main activity of this working farm. The Sheppy family has been making cider since the early 1800s. Visitors can wander through the 42 acre (17 ha) apple orchards among many varieties of cider apple trees.

FARMS
Animal Farm Conservation Reserve, Red Road, Berrow, Burnham-on-Sea. Telephone: 0278 75628.

Enjoy the farm and conservation trail in tranquil surroundings, and the fine collection of vintage farm machinery and hand tools. There are many rare and domestic breeds of farm animals which visitors can feed and make friends with. Light refreshments are normally available.

Higher Folly Farm, Crewkerne. Telephone: 0460 76966.

This is an unusual sheep dairying farm. Sheep's milk has been used for centuries for the production of cheeses and today the range of products has increased to include yoghourts, fudge and frozen milk lollies. The farm is home to the Morton Herd of pedigree British Friesland sheep and supplies sheep milk products throughout south-west England. In the milking parlour visitors can watch the dairy ewes being milked — it is surprising just how much milk they produce.

New Road Farm, New Road, East Huntspill. Telephone: 0278 783250.

There are milking demonstrations daily and feeding routines throughout the day (check for times and details). There is also a Barn Owl Release Scheme. After walking the farm trail and seeing the sixty different breeds of farm animals, visitors can enjoy a cream tea in the delightful 300-year-old farmhouse.

Norwood Farm, Bath Road, Norton St Philip. Telephone: 037387 356.

Visitors are welcome at this mixed, fully organic working farm and rare breed centre where a large number of old native breeds are reared alongside the commercial stock. Fleece

The Wellington Monument.

and wool from Shetland, Portland and Wensleydale sheep, mohair and cashgora from the Angora goats and other produce can be bought at the shop.

Somerset Farm Park, Allerford, Porlock. Telephone: 0643 862816.

The farm was used as a set in the feature film of *Lorna Doone*; it is a traditional place now offering a modern service. The Farm Park houses a menagerie of old English farm animals and birds: pigs, goats, sheep, rabbits and poultry. There are exhibitions of country crafts and old farm implements as well as demonstrations of horse driving and ploughing.

MONUMENTS
King Alfred's Tower, Stourton, Brewham, Wincanton.

King Alfred's Tower stands on King's Settle Hill, commanding an impressive view. It was completed by Henry Hoare in 1772 to commemorate the victory over the Danes by Alfred in AD 879. The tower is 164 feet (50 metres) high with a triangular tower and turret at each angle and the top can be reached by climbing the 121 steps. This is reputed to be the spot were Alfred raised his standard against the Danes, and a memorial plaque at the entrance bears this story.

Wellington Monument, Wellington.

The monument was built between 1817 and 1854 on the high scarp of the Blackdown Hills overlooking Wellington to commemorate the military achievements of the Duke who took his name from the town. Its prominence over the surrounding countryside makes it a familiar landmark to many holidaymakers who travel past but those who care to stop and make the climb are justly rewarded, for the views are quite superb, and the 175 foot (53.3 metre) high grey stone obelisk is impressively massive. There is a distance and direction table to aid the identification of features in the landscape.

RAILWAYS
The East Somerset Railway, Cranmore Railway Station, Shepton Mallet. Telephone: 074988 417.

On the A361 at Cranmore, near Shepton Mallet, the East Somerset Railway has its headquarters in the old country station built in 1858. Here a collection of nine steam locomotives is displayed in a Victorian-style locomotive shed, and at weekends and other days in the summer some of them are steamed down the line. There is a display of prints by David Shepherd, the wildlife artist, in the Signal Box Art Gallery. A brochure is available by post.

The West Somerset Railway at Stogumber.

The West Somerset Railway, The Station, Minehead TA24 5BG. Telephone: 0643 4996.

The West Somerset Railway operates steam trains from Minehead to Bishop's Lydeard on the line which was closed by British Rail in 1971; enthusiastic volunteers and ex-railwaymen reopened it in 1976 after much hard work to create the longest independent railway in Britain. Trains pass through the most beautiful rural and coastal scenery, calling at Dunster, Blue Anchor, Washford, Watchet, Donniford, Williton, Stogumber and Crowcombe. There are various small railway museums at stops down the line, notably at Washford (see chapter 8).

TRADITIONAL CRAFTS

The English Basket Centre, Curload, Stoke St Gregory. Telephone: 0823 69418.

At the heart of the willow-growing area of central Somerset 'The Willow Walk' guides visitors through the various stages of processing the crop — sorting, boiling, stripping — and shows basketmaking in progress. A small proportion of the crop finds its way into enclosed furnaces where artists' charcoal is produced. A good variety of locally made baskets and other willow products is available from the shop.

Peat Moors Visitor Centre, The Willows Peat Company Garden Centre, Shapwick Road, Westhay, near Glastonbury BA6 9TT. Telephone: 04586 257.

Opened in 1986, the Peat Moors Visitor Centre provides an excellent and comprehensive display of information relating to all aspects of the Peat Moors of central Somerset. It is arranged in three sections. First come the fascinating archaeological finds, with photographs of the incredibly well preserved wooden trackways and iron age lake villages which have been discovered in the peat. Various items are on display, and visitors are invited to walk on the reconstruction of the 6000-year-old Sweet Track.

The second section describes the history of peat formation and how and why it has proved to be such an important commodity. Displays illustrate the range of tools used to extract peat, from Victorian spades and peat scythes through to gigantic modern excavators.

The final section, compiled with the help of the Nature Conservancy Council and the RSPB, uses photographs to show the unique flora and fauna that are attracted to the low-lying wet conditions of the Moors.

Adjoining the Garden Centre is a display of traditional turfing, which runs from April to September, showing how peat was cut for fuel and stacked for drying until the advent of machinery in the 1950s. A programme of gardening and local interest tutorials is available throughout the year.

Willows and Wetlands Visitor Centre, P. H. Coate and Son, Meare Green Court, Stoke St Gregory, Taunton TA3 6HY. Telephone: 0823 490249.

A particular feature of low-lying central Somerset is the cultivation of willows for basket and hurdle making and the production of artists' charcoal. Here at Stoke St Gregory, where the traditional methods have been

Stripping willow at the English Basket Centre, Curload.

practised by the Coate family since the early nineteenth century, all aspects of the industry are combined to give a comprehensive and informative display.

All the processes of the industry can be seen, from the planting of the willow sets and their management until harvest-time in mid November. The willows are still cut and bundled by hand, using a hook. The cut withies are taken to the willow-processing yard, where they are sorted according to length and put into smaller bundles ready for the boiling stage. This softens the bark, making it easier to strip; this is now done by a machine, but used to be laboriously tackled, a rod at a time, by local women and children. After boiling, the buff willows are hung out to dry thoroughly before they are tied into bundles once more and are ready for the basketmaker or for processing into charcoal. In the workshop a large variety of Somerset baskets are made to order and for sale in the shop and there is a display of photographs relating to the industry since the nineteenth century.

With the sponsorship of the Countryside Forum an exhibition has been mounted describing the unique nature of the wetlands of Somerset. This reveals, with the aid of photographs, models and drawings, how today's landscape has evolved from marsh and swamp, and details the flora and fauna associated with the area.

VINEYARDS

In recent years there has been a revival of viticulture in Somerset and in good years the wine produced has been favourably compared with the best French wines. Vineyards are nothing new to Somerset: in the fourteenth century the abbot of Glastonbury had several under his jurisdiction to supply wine for his table. The south-facing slopes of the Mendip ridge are particularly suited to viticulture and it is here that the present-day vineyards have been established.

Moorlynch Vineyard, Moorlynch, near Bridgwater. Telephone: 0458 210393.

On the south-facing slopes of the Polden Hills, midway between Glastonbury and Bridgwater, the farm specialises in three principal grape varieties — Muller Thurgau, Madeleine Angevine and Seyval Blanc — planted for the specific purpose of producing a well balanced wine. The first vintage in 1983 yielded a wine which won a national award and the subsequent wines have maintained similar quality. Visitors can explore the 12 acre (4.8 ha) vineyard and the rest of the farm, which includes sheep, pigs, cattle and some rare breeds of poultry, with the pleasure of a wine bar offering light lunches and Moorlynch wine for refreshment.

Pilton Manor Vineyard, Pilton, Shepton Mallet BA4 4BE. Telephone: 074989 325.

This historic vineyard was one originally planted by the Abbots of Glastonbury in 1189, and was replanted in 1966. Here there are wine tastings, lectures, talks and guided tours of the process, and an exhibition of harvesting and winemaking machinery. You can enjoy a glass of wine with your lunch in the restaurant.

Whatley Vineyard, Whatley, near Frome. Telephone: 037384 467.

First planted in 1979, this vineyard extends to 4 acres (1.6 ha) and includes five grape varieties to suit local soils and climate. The winery was established in 1986 and consists of a grape crusher, press, fermentation tanks, filtration equipment and bottler. Winemaking takes place between picking in October and bottling in the spring, but visitors may see the winery throughout the year.

The well stocked walled herb garden is divided by paths in the shape of a cross with the four beds planted with aromatic, medicinal, culinary and cosmetic herbs.

Wootton Vineyard, North Wootton, Shepton Mallet. Telephone: 074989 359.

The emblem or logo of the vineyard is a drawing of a thirteenth-century carving in Wells Cathedral of 'The Grape Stealers'; it is appropriate evidence of the fact that grapes have been grown in this area since medieval times, mostly associated with ecclesiastical estates. The Wootton Vineyard was planted in 1971 in the foothills of the Mendips and it has produced some excellent dry crisp white wines. Tours and wine tastings are offered to groups of more than twenty people.

Wraxall Vineyard, Shepton Mallet. Telephone: 074986 486 or 331.

The vineyard was founded in 1973 and is unusual in the arrangement of the vines, which are trained along wires 5 feet (1.5 metres) high with the annual growth hanging down. The leafy avenues formed between the ranks of vines are unlike anything to be seen in Europe; the technique was pioneered on the eastern coast of the USA. In addition to several crisp white wines, this vineyard also produces a light red wine. Visitors are welcome throughout the year, although there is naturally most to see in the summer and autumn.

WATERMILLS AND WINDMILLS

Chapel Allerton Windmill, near Wedmore. Bristol Museum.

The last windmill to be worked in the county, it was used until 1927. Restored some years ago and presented to Bristol Museum, it stands in beautiful countryside overlooking the low Moors. It is a stone-built tower mill with a revolving cap; the working parts inside are complete.

Clapton Flour Mill, Clapton, Crewkerne TA18 8PU. Telephone: 0460 73124.

Built in 1864, this is the only commercial water-powered flour mill that has continually produced wholemeal flour since 1870, when the Lockyers arrived. The 21 foot (6.4 metre) wheel still drives the machinery. Visitors get a full guided tour, with a good explanation of the machinery, operation and history of the flour-milling process.

Cutterne Mill, Southwood, near Evercreech. See chapter 8.

Dunster Water Mill, Mill Lane, Dunster.

Circle the hill on which Dunster Castle stands, either by the footpath (when the castle is open) to the east or West Street and Mill Lane to the west, and find the Dunster Water Mill. It is a delightful spot hard by the river Avill. The mill is powered by unique twin overshot wheels and is in full working order — stoneground flour milled on the premises is available for purchase.

High Ham Windmill, near Langport TA10 9DJ. Telephone: 0458 250818. National Trust.

Open only by appointment with the tenant, this is a stone windmill with a thatched roof dating from 1822 and in use until 1910. It is set in a magnificent position with views towards High Ham and the Blackdowns and over the low Moors to Brent Knoll.

Hornsbury Mill, near Chard. See chapter 8.

Orchard Mill, Williton. See chapter 8.

Chapel Allerton Windmill.

45

Piles Mill, Allerford.

Piles Mill, Allerford. Information from the National Trust. Telephone: 0643 862452.

This small, quietly situated watermill has an overshot wheel but no original machinery. There is a collection of agricultural bygones.

OTHER ACTIVITIES
The Battle of Sedgemoor and the Pitchfork Rebellion Trail.

Follow the trail by car from Bridport (Dorset), where the Duke of Monmouth landed on 11th June 1685, through many of the towns and villages of Somerset which saw the rise of his rebel army and skirmishes with the Royalist troops, to Westonzoyland and the monument on the site of the battle of Sedgemoor, fought on 6th July 1685. The King's army, surprised by a night attack, successfully turned the tables on the ill equipped rebels and the cavalry pursued the defeated and exhausted West Country men until 700 lay dead and 300 were taken prisoner. The aftermath of trials against the rebels has gone down in history as the Bloody Assizes; Lord Chief Justice Jeffreys sentenced more than 300 men to be hanged and their dismembered corpses were distributed about the West Country for public display. The luckier ones were transported to work as slaves on the plantations of Barbados and other islands of the West Indies. The County Museum in Taunton Castle (where the Taunton Assize was held) and the Admiral Blake Museum in Bridgwater (chapter 8) show exhibitions of relics from the battlefield and rebellion. A leaflet describing the events in more detail and outlining the tour is available from tourist information offices.

Brean Leisure Park, Brean Sands. Telephone: 027875 595.

A pleasure land of fun and games for the family including more than twenty attractions, the park is tucked behind the sand dunes just a couple of hundred yards from the 7 mile (11.2 km) long beach at Brean. The Wet 'N' Wild aquaslide provides extra excitement for swimmers and there are good facilities for young children too. Catering is available at various levels to suit many occasions and in the evening the Farmers' Tavern is a popular local nightspot.

Chewton Cheese Dairy, Priory Farm, Chewton Mendip BA3 4NT. Telephone: 076121 666.

This is a farm where you can watch Cheddar cheese being made by hand, as it used to be. The scale of production has increased enormously — 2500 gallons (11,000 litres) of milk a day — so do not expect a leisurely rural scene. It is, however, a fascinating process and a guide is usually available to describe the whole process and show visitors the cheese maturing in the cheese store.

Cricket St Thomas Wildlife Park, Chard TA20 2DD. Telephone: 046030 755.

See also chapter 7. This beautiful park is set in an area of outstanding natural beauty; in the sheltered valley and lakes a great variety of animals and birds lead a free-roaming life in a superb habitat. Elephants, camels and llamas wander about the old walled gardens and grounds, and in the lake sea-lions provide an entertaining sideshow. Many wild waterfowl augment the introduced species such as flamingoes and swans. The success of the breeding programmes, particularly of the Australian black swans which have become the estate's emblem, are indicative of the general well-being and contentment of the animals. The National Heavy Horse Centre, at the Home Farm, is one of the few places in Britain where these magnificent creatures are still bred. The centre has its own team of heavy horses which give regular demonstrations and make appearances at local shows and carnivals. The country life museum has a fine collection of Victorian dairy and milking equipment. The milking of the modern dairy herd can be seen every afternoon through a viewing window in the walled garden, and the cream is used to produce a delicious ice-cream, on sale with other local food specialities in the farm shop

on the estate.

There is an exciting children's adventure playground, complete with life-size American fort, miniature railway, and assault courses through the woods for the more energetic, whilst the picnic area and cafe facilities cater for those who prefer more leisurely pursuits.

Westonzoyland Pumping Station, Westonzoyland.

Drainage of one sort or another has created the landscape of central Somerset and allowed its use for agriculture. The first steam pumping station in the county was built in Westonzoyland in 1830 to pump water from the rhyne, or ditch, into the river Parrett. The original beam engine and scoop wheel were soon found to be inadequate and in 1861 the existing Easton and Amos drainage machine was installed. That engine and other associated machinery are being restored and can be seen working. Visitors can watch (and occasionally help) the blacksmith in his forge. There is also a narrow-gauge contractor's railway once used by the Somerset River Authority.

Above: *Sedgemoor battlefield with a diorama of the site.*

Right: *Westonzoyland Pumping Station.*

The thatched stack of hurdles at Priddy.

10
Customs and special events

Somerset is a county rich in rural traditions, fairs and shows and a surprising number of its folklore customs can still be enjoyed. Full details can be obtained from tourist information centres (chapter 13).

JANUARY
Plough Monday
Several rural parishes celebrate this event. Originally farm labourers paraded through the village hauling a plough decorated with ribbons. A mumming play was the usual entertainment.

Wassailing
This delightful custom was designed to ensure a copious crop of apples (for cidermaking) the following season. The Somerset Rural Life Museum at Glastonbury wassails the trees in its orchards and several pubs have revived the festival, notably the Butchers' Arms at Carhampton and the Pike and Musket at Walton, near Street. Wassailing involves scaring the evil spirits out of the apple orchard, encouraging the good spirits (with plenty of cider) and singing a song:

'Old apple tree, old apple tree
We've come to wassail thee.
To bear and bow apples enow,
Hats full, caps full,
Three bushel bags full,

Barn floors full and a
Little heap under the stairs.'

FEBRUARY
Egg Shackling
Some country schools have retained this game, usually on Shrove Tuesday. Eggs identified by a mark or tag are shaken in a sieve. Those that remain unbroken longest are the winners.

APRIL
Candle auctions
A candle auction is still held at Tatworth, near Chard, although it is not generally open to the public. The aim is to auction a plot of land and a watercress bed. This is done by fixing about an inch (25 mm) of a tallow candle to a board suspended from the ceiling so that the bidders can see only the glow of its flame. The last bidder before the candle goes out is the holder of the land for the following year.

MAY
Hobby Horse Festival, Minehead.
An ancient festival, probably celebrating the end of the winter and practised throughout Europe and at Padstow in Cornwall, this is the highlight of the Somerset folklore year. The 'horse' is kept throughout the year at the Queen's Head Inn. It appears on the eve of

May Day and on May Day itself and dances through the streets to the accompaniment of pipes, drum and accordion. The horse is joined by 'gullivers' or attendants at a road junction called the Cher and there the 'booting' takes place. It is well worth a visit.

JUNE
Sheep shearing
You will be lucky to find anyone celebrating the completion of shearing today with a 'bowl of furmity' and a feast for their workers. The festival dates from a time when the whole community joined in:

'Wife make us a dinner, spare flesh neither corne,
Make wafers and cakes, for our sheepe must be shorne,
At sheep shearing, neighbours none other things crave,
But good cheers and welcome like neighbours to have.'

Royal Bath and West Show
Now held at the permanent showground just outside Shepton Mallet, this is one of the oldest agricultural shows in Britain. In 1977 it celebrated its bicentenary with a visit from the Prince of Wales. It is a huge event, impressively organised with marquees, show tents, pavilions, ring events and livestock.

AUGUST
Harvest Home
Many villages organise a harvest home dinner, usually a mainly private event, but sometimes linked with a fair or dancing. Wedmore and East Brent have particularly colourful celebrations with massive marquees and a handsome luncheon for the villagers.

Priddy Fair
Throughout the year a pile of hurdles under a thatched roof sits on Priddy Green, a permanent reminder of the invasion of sheep at this summer fair when for one hectic day the village is packed with people, animals and activity. The fair was transferred to Priddy from Wells on account of the plague in 1348. This fair takes place in August, usually on or about the 21st, and is a pleasure to visit because of its country atmosphere. There is a local proverb that 'the first rain after Priddy Fair is the first rain of winter'.

SEPTEMBER
Yesterday's Farming
The annual event of the South Somerset Agricultural Preservation Society takes place at a different location each year on the first weekend in September. It is a two-day event with a truly rural atmosphere. On the Saturday there are usually processions of ancient tractors and tractor-drawn machinery, an array of hissing and puffing stationary engines and demonstrations of steam-driven threshing machines and saw benches. On the Sunday heavy horses are the central attraction, and there are said to be more here than at any other event in the South-west. There are horse ploughing competitions, harness displays and a magnificent procession of heavy horses around the ring. Sideshows of traditional rural crafts, morris dancing and sheepdog trials complete the country atmosphere.

St Matthew's Fair, Bridgwater.
As early as the fourteenth century, this fair was making a profit and it has continued successfully to the present day. It was a hiring fair, when men and women seeking work lined up to be hired, their contracts running from one fair time to another. The old Somerset word 'mop' for a fair probably has its origin in this custom, as the maidservants used to carry a mop as a symbol of their work. The fair is now held on the last Wednesday of September and the following three days. The first day is 'James Day', when the fair field throngs with sheep and hill ponies for sale. Nowadays it is the funfair that attracts the crowds, together with the stalls and sideshows.

OCTOBER
St Crispin's Day
St Crispin is the patron saint of shoe workers, hence the celebration of this day in Street, the home of Clarks' shoes. The local church is still sometimes decorated with shoes and a special service of thanksgiving held.

Punky Night
The last Thursday in October is the occasion for this festival still held at the little village of Hinton St George. Children make up grotesque lanterns carved out of mangolds and chant the traditional song:

'Gie us a candle, gie us a light,
It's Punky Night tonight.
It's Punky Night tonight.
Adam and Eve wouldn't believe,
It's Punky Night tonight.'

NOVEMBER
Carnival week
This is the highlight of the year for many clubs and societies throughout central Somerset. Bridgwater is always the first venue, on the nearest Thursday to Guy Fawkes Day. Then the floats block the roads daily as they are moved on a circuit of the other towns — North Petherton, Highbridge, Burnham-on-Sea, Shepton Mallet, Midsomer Norton, Wells, Glastonbury and finally Weston-super-Mare. The carnival begins in each town at about 7 pm, the pavements are packed with

sightseers and street vendors, and the atmosphere buzzes with anticipation until the floats appear.

The carnival procession in Bridgwater is the largest. It attracts thousands of visitors every year, and the brightly illuminated floats take up to two hours to pass by. The floats are extraordinary creations, often massive in scale, with a 'King Kong' or 'Mexican bandit', perhaps 20 feet (6 metres) high, carefully constructed in timber and papier-mâché, garishly painted and festooned with light bulbs. Dressed in an array of colourful costumes, the members of the Carnival Clubs dance, pose or sing to booming music as they vie for originality and splendour. It is said that the best clubs start to plan for the following year as soon as the current show is over. After the procession a Squibbing Display is held in the High Street. Men from each 'gang' shoulder a long wooden handle to which is attached a 'Bridgwater Squib'. These huge fireworks burn for several minutes, sending fountains of fire as high as the rooftops, finally exploding stars into the night sky.

DECEMBER
Ashen Faggot Ceremony

The Luttrell Arms, Dunster, has revived this event, but the night varies from Christmas Eve to New Year's Eve in different parts of the county and there is no guarantee that you will find it taking place. The ceremony consists of burning a faggot-bundle of wood bound with willow bands. Everyone is meant to take a drink as each band burns and breaks in the fire.

King John's Hunting Lodge at Axbridge.

Admiral Blake's statue in Bridgwater.

The river Parrett at Bridgwater.

11
Towns and villages

AXBRIDGE
Early closing Wednesday.

On the north-western edge of the Mendip Hills, Axbridge looks out across the low-lying plains of central Somerset towards the Wedmore ridge and Polden Hills. The town is dwarfed by the limestone cliff which rises behind it. Though only just off the A38 and not far from the motorway, Axbridge has remained unspoilt and retains old-world charm and interest. It is a quiet place; the once active Market Square has become a small but central car park and the limited fringe development peters out towards the Moors, where the land scarcely rises above sea level.

The principal feature of Axbridge is its twisting High Street, following its medieval path and flanked by some fascinating medieval buildings. These are, for the most part, timber-framed and timber building is unusual in Somerset. King John's Hunting Lodge, at the corner of the High Street and the Square, is the best example, beautifully restored by the National Trust and open to the public as a local museum (see chapter 8).

The old Market Square is overlooked by the parish church of St John the Baptist, up a dented flight of steps. The church is mainly fifteenth-century, with an excellent brass to Roger Harper and his wife (late fourteenth century) of 'big, stiff kneeling figures, and outside them a curious breed of half angels, half quite attractive mermaids'. Also in the

Square notice the amusing *trompe l'oeil* window above the town hall. The old workhouse, now a hospital, is an impressive, if austere, building and the old railway station, strangely isolated now on the bypass, has become a youth club.

BRIDGWATER
Early closing Thursday; market day Wednesday.

The town developed at the lowest crossing point of the river Parrett, where the fertile plains of central Somerset meet the Severn estuary. It is an important commercial and industrial centre, with a lively market serving the agricultural community. Even in the seventeenth century Bridgwater was described as 'a well-to-do place with a thriving coast trade carried on down the river'. In the nineteenth century the opening of the Bridgwater to Taunton canal reinforced its economic status, and in 1841 the Bristol and Exeter Railway Company opened an impressive new docks and warehouse complex. Virtually all Bridgwater's medieval buildings have been lost to recent developments. There was once a central castle dominating the river crossing (at the top of Castle Street), a friary and a medieval hospital.

The river divides the town into two. In 1795 an iron bridge spanned the muddy banks of the Parrett, one of the earliest iron bridges in Britain, made by Abraham Darby of Coalbrookdale; it was removed in 1883 because it was too hump-backed and the present bridge was installed. On the east side lie most of the factories, the railway station and the market. Here were the famous Barham's brick and tile yards which supplied much of the county with plain bricks, pantiles and decorated roof finials. The remains of one bottle kiln can still be seen.

On the west bank the principal shopping streets radiate from the Cornhill, where Admiral Blake's statue stands. In a car park adjoining the old docks the remains of a glass kiln are visible, built by the Duke of Chandos, who also built the finest street in the town, Castle Street. Number 11 Castle Street has the distinction of having been the first arts centre in Britain, opened in 1946 by the Arts Council. It was once visited by Picasso and now includes a theatre and exhibition gallery. Blake's birthplace is now a museum (see chapter 8).

Bridgwater is one of Somerset's most industrialised towns: British Cellophane and Clarks (shoes) have large factories, and there are many smaller firms.

BRUTON
Early closing Thursday.

Bruton is a picturesque and unspoilt little town on the river Brue, midway between Frome and Yeovil. The quality of the ancient stone buildings lining the main street and the atmosphere of genteel decay suggest past splendour; this was one of the royal boroughs created by the Saxon kings of Wessex. At the time of Canute there was even a royal mint here.

Just downstream from the road bridge over the river is a beautifully arched packhorse bridge called the Little Bow; it was built in the fifteenth century, when pony trains laden with woollen goods tramped from this area down to the south coast ports. The church is unusual in having two towers. The shorter one was built in the fourteenth century, the other about a hundred years later. Inside notice the tomb of Sir Maurice Berkely with his two wives, Elizabeth Sandys and Katharine Blount. The High Street is narrow; on the south side even narrower 'bartons' or alleys slip between the tall buildings down to the river. There are a handful of shops, several interesting old houses and a host of antique and junk shops worth investigating.

On the hill south of the town the strange tower that looks like a folly was the dovecote, or *columbarium,* of Bruton Priory. Pigeons were kept here to provide the prior and his followers with fresh meat throughout the year. Another remnant of the Priory is the great high buttressed wall west of the church, built, apparently, to hide the monks from public view. Today the wall hides part of the King's

School, founded in 1519 by various city gentlemen including Richard Fitzjames, Bishop of London. Sexey's Hospital was built in the seventeenth century by the trustees of the founder, Hugh Sexey. It looks like the court of an Oxbridge college. Sexey was Auditor of the Exchequer to Elizabeth I.

BURNHAM-ON-SEA
Early closing Wednesday.

Although Burnham is only a small town, the built-up area extends some 6 miles (9.6 km) north up the coast towards Brean Down. The development is made up of holiday camps, caravan parks, apartments, camp sites and amusement areas bordering the sand dunes and the beach.

There are few traces of the farming community from which the town grew. The fifteenth-century church near the sea front has a slight list, being built on sandy soil too close to the shore. It is extraordinary that the remains of the Whitehall Altar, commissioned by James II from Grinling Gibbons in 1686 for the Whitehall Palace, have ended up here. In the summer, Burnham is crowded with visitors: there is said to be a turnover of about twenty thousand a week. There are excellent holiday facilities, including a golf course, fishing, sailing and swimming.

CASTLE CARY
Early closing Thursday.

A quiet country town south of the Mendip Hills, set in the gentle countryside of southeast Somerset, Castle Cary is surrounded by green pastures and wooded hedgerows. The castle was stormed by King Stephen in 1138 and now only the rectangle of the keep marks its position on the hill north-east of the church. The church, with a spire, which is unusual in Somerset, has a fine peal of eight bells. In the middle of the town is the old market hall. It has a clock, and lions holding up the roof. Half of it now belongs to an agricultural merchant, the other half is a tiny museum (see chapter 8). Behind the hall on Bailey Hill is the old circular lock-up, called the Pepper Pot, built in 1779 for £23. There are only four like it in Britain. It is 7 feet (2.1 metres) in diameter and 10 feet (3 metres) high, with two little iron grilles for ventilation.

CHARD
Early closing Wednesday.

On the main A30 route from London to Exeter, Chard is a small but thriving town on the southern border of Somerset. It is surrounded by undulating, unspoilt countryside and is within easy reach of the south coast resorts of Dorset and Devon. As a town with considerable light manufacturing and service industries it has expanded and prospered in

Burnham-on-Sea.

recent years.

Chard was founded as a 'new' town in 1234 by Bishop Jocelyn of Wells. Its economy thrived on its woollen industry and by the sixteenth century Chard cloth was being exported to France. Some of the rich clothiers' houses can still be seen in the High Street. Eighteenth-century weavers' cottages survive both there and in Holyrood Street. In the nineteenth century the cottage-based woollen industry suffered and eventually collapsed owing to competition from the mechanised spinning and weaving mills of the north of England. Chard recovered with a variety of new activities such as making nets and lace and agricultural machinery. Denings, one of the local foundries, invented and manufactured an impressive array of horse-drawn farm machines and hand tools. Chard's potato market was said to be the largest in England.

For a brief time Chard even had a canal. The Chard Canal Company was founded in 1834 and built a canal from the town northwards towards Creech St Michael and Taunton, where it joined the canal to Bridgwater. It was bought out in 1866 by the Bristol and Exeter Railway Company but that was only a little more successful. Chard found itself at an awkward junction between the Great Western Railway's broad gauge and the London and South Western's standard gauge. Eventually the problem was solved in 1891, when the entire 13 mile (21 km) Great Western line to Taunton was converted. In 1966 the railway deserted Chard altogether.

Chard High Street has retained much of historical interest, including the magnificent Guildhall, the Choughs Hotel and Manor Court House. More recent buildings worth finding are the Baptist Chapel in Holyrood Street and, reminders of the industrial past, two mills complete with ironwork of the 1820s. The museum is at the west end of the High Street and nearby is Hornsbury Mill, a popular attraction (see chapter 8).

CHEDDAR

A deep fracture in the limestone mass that forms the Mendips high above Cheddar has created the famous gorge which attracts huge numbers of visitors to this small town. As the road winds down the chasm it is almost engulfed by the towering cliffs on either side — bare rock faces, which rise almost vertically to 1000 feet (304 metres). It is a dramatic and awe-inspiring approach to a once delightful small settlement. Commercialisation has taken its toll, however, and as the gorge widens at the southern end there is an alarming array of souvenir and gift shops and endless ice-cream booths and cafes to cater for the hungry tourists. The underground scenery is as dramatic as the gorge. The scale of the underground chambers and the magnificence of the geological features are breathtaking.

The town straggles southwards towards the A371 and it was here, by the church and the river Yeo, that the original settlement developed; the outlines of the Saxon royal palace of Cheddar, associated with King Alfred, can be seen in the grounds of the Kings of Wessex School. The market cross at the road junction was a preacher's cross around which the hexagonal colonnade was built in the sixteenth century, converting it into a market centre where travelling merchants paid rent to sit under cover. In a modern factory-style building there are daily demonstrations of making the world famous cheese that takes its name from the town; cheese from Cheddar was acknowledged to be among the finest in Britain as early as the seventeenth century.

CREWKERNE
Early closing Thursday.

Crewkerne is a country town set in the fork of a valley near the Devon and Dorset borders. The Victorian market hall is at the centre of the town where the roads converge. Market Street contains most of the shops, built in local stone with pantiled roofs. The church of St Bartholomew (see chapter 6) has a medieval roof supported by stone angels. The tower is an impressive 80 feet (24 metres) high and contains eight bells: the nearby pub is called the Five Bells because until 1820 there were only five.

Crewkerne is known particularly for the production of high-quality sailcloth, canvas and webbing. Here sails were made for the Royal Navy in the nineteenth century and the industry has continued. Crewkerne Textiles today manufacture webbing for the Services, nylon twine and sailcloth. Just over the railway bridge south of the town is the little village of **Misterton.** Helen Matthews, who wrote the Victorian classic *Coming through the Rye*, was born here. Youngs of Misterton act as agents for all manner of hunting and trapping devices; many of their traps were invented and first made in their workshop on the edge of the town. The Hong Kong police buy their traps for catching wild cats from Youngs.

DULVERTON
Early closing Thursday.

'Sequestered in a circling dell,
Embraced with forest and with fell,
A vision fair to gaze upon,
Reclines thy vale, O Dulverton.'
(Reverend F. Tilney Basset, 1874.)

On the boundary between the wilds of Exmoor and the rich countryside of the Brendon Hills, Dulverton shelters in the deeply cut valley of the river Barle. Today it is a small and picturesque town, popular with summer visitors. The five-arched bridge over the river is an ancient monument. Nearby is the old workhouse, now Exmoor House, the headquarters of the National Park, where leaflets and information are available.

In the town, there are two good eighteenth-century inns complete with cobbled yards. It was in one of these, perhaps, that John Ridd of *Lorna Doone* ordered his 'hot mootton pasty with gravy' when travelling back from his school in Tiverton. The magnificent scenery, the fishing and the walks in the surrounding hills make Dulverton an ideal centre for an active holiday.

DUNSTER
Early closing Wednesday.

The village sits under wooded hills at the head of the beautiful Avill valley, dominated by the battlements of Dunster Castle (see chapter 5). It is a nearly perfect example of a medieval village that has survived almost unaltered. At the opposite end of the wide main street from the castle is an octagonal yarn market, built in 1609 by George Luttrell; here a local cloth, described as a soft kersey and called 'Dunsters', was sold. The Nunnery in Church Street has an unusual front elevation with its two upper storeys tile-hung, locally called 'fish-scale' or 'pan-tiling'. Nearby there is a unique example of a thirteenth-century dovecote which belonged to the monks of Dunster Priory. It is a circular stone building with a revolving wooden ladder inside to give access to the five hundred holes for nests built into the walls. The fifteenth-century priory church of St George has a superb wagon roof and is famous for its tuneful bells.

On a hill beside the castle (called Conygar: the old coney warren of the castle), another tower can be seen rising from the woods. It is a folly designed in 1776 for the Luttrells by Richard Phelps; the expenses for building it included £54 for the workmen's cider!

Below the castle, at the end of Mill Lane, is Dunster Water Mill. This is an original seventeenth-century working mill with unusual twin

The cross at Cheddar.

Dulverton Market House.

overshot wheels; stoneground wholemeal flour can be bought from the mill (see chapter 9).

EXFORD

Located at the heart of the National Park, Exford can justify its claim to be the 'capital' of Exmoor. It is a pleasant village of cottages and small hotels around an open triangular green; at the apex of the triangle the old ford has been replaced by a bridge over the river Exe. Exford is the headquarters of the Exmoor Hunt and in the season steaming horses and weary riders seek refreshment in the river and pubs respectively. There are ranks of stables behind both the Crown and White Horse hotels and the staghounds are kennelled nearby.

The church is set high on a hill, away from the village. The base and shaft are all that remains of a Saxon cross in the churchyard. The church itself dates largely from the sixteenth century, when great improvements were made by the rector, George Elsworthy. The fifteenth-century rood screen was originally in St Audries church near Watchet; it was installed here in 1929. The choir stalls were brought from Queens' College, Cambridge. By the churchyard gate, a stone cross marks the grave of Amos Cann; he was caught in a snowstorm in the winter of 1891 while walking home from Porlock to Exford and froze to death. It was three weeks before his body was found.

FROME

Early closing Thursday; market days Wednesday and Saturday.

Frome is the best of the Mendip towns; like all of them it suffered nearly two centuries of decline after the eclipse of the local woollen industry. Frome is full of charm and fascination, with a surprise around every corner. The town is closely packed on a steep hillside, with narrow streets and tight lanes weaving up and down the slopes. The numerous eighteenth-century merchants' houses and weavers' cottages illustrate the prosperity of the place at that time, when its population rivalled that of Bath and Salisbury. Sadly, by 1826 the decline had set in and William Cobbett described it thus: 'I saw between two and three hundred weavers, men and boys, cracking stones . . . these poor creatures at Frome have pawned all their things . . . their blankets and sheets, their looms.'

The market place is near the bridge over the river Frome, which tumbles through the valley. Notice the eighteenth-century facade of the Bluecoat School with its stone figures of a schoolboy and schoolgirl above the doorway. The most picturesque lane in Frome is Cheap Street, for pedestrians only, with a rushing

The Abbot's Fish House at Meare.

conduit down the middle and flanked by small shops and cafes. On the other side of the main road the maze of narrow streets continues. There are numerous antique and junk shops, second-hand bookshops and small craft workshops. Sheppard's Barton, through an arch off Catherine Hill, is a rare street of eighteenth-century workers' cottages, with the Manse at one end from which the mill owner could keep an eye on his employees. Local history is well represented in the museum in North Parade (see chapter 8).

St John's church was heavily restored in the nineteenth century, but traces of Saxon masonry from the church possibly built by St Aldhelm are incorporated in one of the walls and underneath the tower (see chapter 6). The Merlins Theatre in the suburbs offers a lively selection of entertainment and exhibitions.

GLASTONBURY
Early closing Wednesday; market day Tuesday.

From whichever direction you approach Glastonbury it will be the famous Tor that you first see and it is easy to imagine how so dramatic a landmark acquired such mystical significance. On a misty morning, when the moors are shrouded by a white haze, the summit of the Tor and the brittle tower of St Michael's Chapel appear to be floating, as if on a lake. Maybe that is how it seemed to earlier inhabitants when the moors were frequently inundated by the sea. The town has grown up at the foot of the Tor, just above the area liable to flooding and around the ancient site of the abbey ruins (see chapters 4 and 5).

Glastonbury is a small market town largely dependent on the summer visitors who flock to the abbey in large numbers. Driving through, the initial impression is not very exciting, but behind the modern shop fronts and car park signs there is a wealth of history and interest to be discovered. Several medieval buildings survive outside the abbey precincts, most notably the Tribunal and Abbey Barn (now both museums, see chapter 8), the George and Pilgrims Inn, St Mary's Almshouses and the two churches, St John's and St Benedict's. Students of legend and folklore are offered 'mystic' tours to see the Holy Thorn and Weary-all Hill, where Joseph of Arimathea is said to have planted his staff. Chalice Well and its neatly kept gardens are open to the public near the footpath which leads up the Tor.

In the eighteenth century Glastonbury enjoyed a short-lived tourist boom as a spa town. The former pump rooms, built in 1754, survive as a private house next to the Copper Beech Hotel in Magdalene Street. Through an archway beside the High Street notice the Assembly Rooms (built in 1864) where Rutland Boughton first presented *The Immortal Hour* and Bernard Shaw was entertained.

ILCHESTER
Lindinis was an important Roman town founded where the great Fosse Way from Axmouth in Devon to Lincoln was crossed by a road from the Bristol Channel to Dorchester at a ford across the river Yeo. All that remains visible today of the once great Roman town

is a few humps in a field, but archaeologists have discovered extensive remains of a walled town, a centre for administration, and the headquarters of a garrison.

From the twelfth century the county jail was located in the town, and this, together with an important market here, gave Ilchester the status of county town for a short time. The jail seemed to dominate activities in the town from the middle ages until the nineteenth century, but sadly the site has now been taken over by a petrol station, although part of its laundry and bakehouse still survive as cottages. To the north of the church, facing the green, there remains a handful of elegant Georgian houses, a small reminder of the town's past glory; large numbers of these houses were demolished to make way for the A303, which now, somewhat ironically, bypasses the town altogether.

The roar of jets from the Royal Naval Air Station at Yeovilton, about a mile east of Ilchester, jolts this peaceful and historic town into the twentieth century. Within the aerodrome is the Fleet Air Arm Museum (see chapter 8), opened by the Duke of Edinburgh in 1964.

ILMINSTER
Early closing Thursday.

Ilminster is an unspoilt and delightfully rural town, the old 'minster' on the river Isle. The main road now takes all the through traffic so the charming market place with its stone-pillared, open-sided market hall is a peaceful spot where the honey-coloured Ham stone glows with warmth and the locals, in true country fashion, pause to chat. The minster, the parish church of St Mary, is an impressive memorial to the town's prosperity in the fourteenth and fifteenth centuries (see chapter 6).

Nicholas Wadham, the founder of Wadham College, Oxford, is buried here, having died before he was able to complete his building; he left the 'whole menagerie' of the college to his wife, Dorothy, who is now buried beside him.

In the eighteenth century Ilminster was at the centre of a network of turnpike roads, linking it with the surrounding towns. There were tollgates at Haslewell, where the gate-house is easily recognisable, and at Cross, Kingstone, Whitelackington, Old Way Gate and the Catherine Wheel. In the nineteenth century the Chard Canal passed just to the west of the town and brought with it a flurry of activity which diminished when the railway arrived in 1866. Just off the main road to the east of the town is Dillington House, a small country estate set in attractive parkland; it is now run by Somerset County Council as an adult education centre. The stable block has been converted into an attractive small

theatre, adjacent to the Butlin Gallery.

LANGPORT

Situated at the tidal limit of the river Parrett, Langport was for centuries a small but important centre for traffic sailing upstream into the heart of Somerset and downstream to Bridgwater. The market that developed here was a reflection of the products from the surrounding moors and marshes. In winter large numbers of fowl were sold, together with eels from the river and moorland rhines or drainage ditches. Down and feathers were also an important commodity, plucked from the flocks of geese that grazed the nearby fields.

The oldest part of the town is up on the hill where there were extensive fortifications and embankments; the barrel-vaulted Eastern Gate still remains, with the 'Hanging Chapel' above. The church of All Saints was rebuilt in the fifteenth century but retains a stone relief of Norman design over the south door. The town is built almost entirely of grey blue Lias stone, which is rather drab and cold, but there are several distinctive houses, most notably in Bow Street and Cheapside. Langport's most famous son, Walter Bagehot (1826-77), economist, banker and author of *The English Constitution*, was born at the house with the

Langport's 'Hanging Chapel'.

plaque in Bow Street, adjacent to the bank founded by his family, the Stuckeys, in about 1770. When the bank was taken over by the National Westminster in 1909 its banknote circulation was second only to that of the Bank of England.

Kelways Nursery, established in 1815, on the edge of the town, is a profusion of colour in the spring and it is renowned for its beautiful peonies and gladioli.

MINEHEAD
Early closing Wednesday.

Sheltered from the brisk westerly winds by densely wooded North Hill, Minehead spreads out beside its sandy beach and esplanade. On the north-eastern edge of Exmoor, it is the largest of the west Somerset coastal resorts and offers many recreational facilities, good hotels and guest houses. As early as 1800 the town attracted 'persons of fashion' with its mild climate and sea air. Today the same attractions bring thousands every week during the summer season, especially to the holiday camp nearby.

Minehead grew up around its quay, which offered safety and shelter on an exposed and hazardous coastline. Higher Town, around the church of St Michael, on the slopes of North Hill, retains much of its charm, with thatched cottages and quaint alleys wriggling up the hillside. Church Steps is a favourite haunt of local artists. Lower or Middle Town is where modern urban development and the shopping centre have taken over on the flatter land. The original buildings were destroyed by a 'deplorable public calamity', a fire, in 1791.

OARE

This remote hamlet was made famous by R. D. Blackmore in his great tale of Exmoor, *Lorna Doone*. The diminutive square-towered church attracts visitors because it was here that Lorna, in her wedding dress of 'pure white, clouded with faint lavender', was shot by Carver Doone just as John Ridd was about to seal their marriage with a kiss. Visitors will search in vain, however, for Plover Barrows Farm, John's home. The church bears a simple memorial to Blackmore; a portrait in a medallion.

Oare is surrounded by mile after mile of rolling moorland; a wild landscape in winter, but a delight for walkers and naturalists at other times of the year. Doone Valley and Badgworthy Water, despite their ominous roles in the story, are wonderful places, with wind-twisted trees, rough grassland, purple heather and a blaze of bright yellow gorse.

PORLOCK

Nestling in the shelter of towering hills, Porlock has somehow managed to escape the ravages of the twentieth century and retains its old-world charm and character, with narrow winding streets, thatched roofs and tall rounded chimneys on solid square bases. The seaward side of the village is bounded by the

Minehead station, terminus of the West Somerset Railway.

Selworthy church.

marsh, confined by a broad crescent of grey shingle. Porlock once had a harbour of its own, at a place the Saxons called 'the enclosure by the harbour', but nowadays boats seek shelter about 1½ miles (2.4 km) to the west, at a little village called Porlock Weir.

The parish church of St Dubricius, in the centre of the village, dates from the thirteenth century; the spire lost its top in a thunderstorm in the seventeenth century. The figure of Sir Simon Fitzroger, who contributed to the building of the church, lies in full armour under a richly carved canopy, whilst the effigy of John Harrington, who fought at Agincourt, is finely chiselled in alabaster, with his wife's beside him, complete with a mitred head-dress with intricate lacework.

SELWORTHY

An entire picture-book village preserved by the National Trust as part of its Holnicote Estate, Selworthy clings to the side of a steep hill looking south over Exmoor. The thatched, whitewashed cottages were built in 1810 by the tenth Holnicote baronet, Sir Thomas Acland, as retirement homes for faithful retainers of the estate workforce. They are grouped picturesquely around a communal green with interconnecting paths and attractive planting. The hillside behind the village was planted with groups of trees by Sir Thomas. Starting in 1809, he planted a group to celebrate the birth of each of his nine children. Holnicote House, used as a holiday home by the Aclands, has burnt down three times since the end of the eighteenth century.

Most of the estate was given to the National Trust by Sir Richard Dyke Acland in 1944, and the house is now used as a holiday centre.

The fifteenth-century church has a square embattled west tower and possesses a fine wagon roof, richly decorated with angels, bosses, shields and symbols.

SHEPTON MALLET
Early closing Wednesday; market day Friday.

Old Shepton surrounds the crossing point over the little river Sheppey, which twists and turns its way through the foothills of the Mendip plateau. The towns developed on the rolling hillsides and the pretty market place slopes steeply down to the river. The surrounding countryside is some of the most attractive in eastern Somerset.

The economy of the town was originally based on its wool-manufacturing industry. Like most of the towns and villages in this part of Somerset, it suffered a decline in the early nineteenth century and has never quite recovered, although the town has benefited from new industries brought here by Showerings (Babycham) and Clarks (shoes), and from brewing; the magnificent shell of the Anglo-Bavarian Brewery building can still be seen from Commercial Road. The old market place has been carefully modernised and a new centre has been built, comprising a theatre, ballroom and restaurants, around which the life of the town carries on much as it did before. The market cross was rebuilt in 1841. Next to it stands a traditional roofed market stall called a 'scamel' or 'shambles'.

59

Shepton Mallet market cross.

SOMERTON
Early closing Wednesday.

An attractive small town built of the local Blue Lias stone, Somerton lies on a ridge overlooking Sedgemoor. It is off the main roads, and consequently it is remarkably quiet and unspoilt. Its claim to be the 'ancient capital of Wessex' is founded more on folklore than fact, although the Ridge was part of the estates of the Saxon royal house.

The medieval borough was granted a weekly market and an annual fair, when horses, cattle, sheep and pigs were lined up in Broad Street and Cow Square and the market place was packed with traders' stalls. In the centre of the market place is a battlemented seventeenth-century market cross and the town hall is surrounded by elegant town houses and old inns. The White Hart is of medieval origin, with traces of the old castle in the masonry of its cellars. The long frontage of the Red Lion in Broad Street is particularly grand, and the whole street has the style of a city boulevard lined with trees. Close to the square are an excellent bakery, a delicatessen and a bookshop.

STREET
Early closing Wednesday.

This is the home town of Clarks' shoes, where Cyrus Clark first established an out-work system and later factory production in the nineteenth century. Street is still dominated by the austere grey stone buildings the company erected to house its machinery and its workforce. The curves of the Henry Moore bronze beside the main factory soften the impression a little.

The Quaker influence of the Clark family prohibited licensed premises within the town until quite recently. Even now there are few public houses in the town centre. Culture was encouraged, though, and Street benefited from the generous paternalism of the shoemakers. Today there are two swimming pools, a theatre, a large library, a technical college and a new shopping centre.

There are bargain 'seconds' in shoe shops in the High Street, fresh from the factory, and the excellent Shoe Museum in the old factory building (see chapter 8).

TAUNTON
Early closing Thursday; market day Saturday.

Somerset's county town lies in the fertile Vale of Taunton Deane where the river Tone meanders lazily across green meadows. It is a proud and spacious town, with a modern shopping centre and wide streets. Although there is some light industry on the outskirts, it is essentially an administrative centre, with County Hall dominating employment.

Since the thirteenth century Taunton has acted as a market and trading centre for this prosperous region. The castle (see chapter 5), possibly of Saxon origin, protected the inhabitants and encouraged peaceful activity. The town never featured strongly in national history, its only claim to fame being the trial of Monmouth's supporters here after the battle of Sedgemoor. The market still attracts traders from a wide area; the livestock market is important to the surrounding farmers, and even if you do not want to buy a heifer or piglet it is well worth a visit, just for the intense atmosphere and the faces of the farmers round the ring. Taunton is well provided with amenities: an indoor swimming pool, landscaped parks and gardens, a library, the County Museum in the castle (see chapter 8), the Brewhouse Theatre (next to the river, and offering delicious salad lunches) and the Somerset County Cricket Club. There is a good selection of hotels and inns. The churches of St James and St Mary Magdalene are described in chapter 6.

TEMPLECOMBE
Early closing Saturday.

The village of Templecombe lies in the

valley of the river Stour and has an historical association with the Knights Templar. They acquired the manor in the twelfth century and founded a preceptory for members of their order. Remains of the old Templar buildings are still to be seen at the Manor House.

Templecombe has an extraordinary and unlikely link in the chain of evidence for the authenticity of the Turin Shroud. During a gale in 1951 an outhouse ceiling in a cottage in the High Street collapsed revealing a panel in the roof covered with coal dust. The panel proved to be a life-size painting, medieval in style, of the head of Christ. It has been suggested that the similarity of this painting, dated to the thirteenth century, to the Shroud's image of Christ supports the theory that the Templars obtained the highly prized Shroud on one of their crusades and brought it back to Europe. A detailed account of the painting and its connection with the Templars can be found in *The Turin Shroud* by Ian Wilson, published in 1978.

WATCHET
Early closing Wednesday.

Watchet is an old fishing port with the atmosphere of Dylan Thomas's *Under Milk Wood*. The harbour, deep in grey mud at low tide, enjoys plenty of activity with all manner of cargoes from shirts to tractor parts.

Watchet was ravaged by Viking raiders who frequently attacked this coastline and carried off or murdered the inhabitants. Because of its value as a harbour the site was fortified by Alfred and by the middle ages it had grown into one of the more important towns in the county — it even had its own mint. In the

nineteenth century Robert Pole and William Wood established a paper mill in the town that is still working today. Van Heusen, the shirt makers, also have a factory here. In the past, when times were hard, the locals took a boat over to Wales to work in the mines, and some engineering firms, like Chidgey's Millwrights, did almost as much work in Wales as they did in Somerset.

The town has a quaint charm and a small museum (see chapter 8). It has not suffered much development and the light industrial aspect of the place seems to have kept down the number of visitors.

WEDMORE
Wedmore lies on the sheltered side of the ridge that runs west from Wells, eventually petering out at Mark. On either side stretch the low level Moors, rich verdant pastures fringed by pollarded willows and rhines. From Wedmore, the grey line of the Mendips looks like a gaunt cliff.

It was here that the Peace of Wedmore was agreed in 878 between King Alfred and the newly baptised Danish leader, Guthrum (see chapter 4), although the nature of the settlement here at that time is uncertain. A great part of the parish church dates from the twelfth century, the most magnificent feature being the south doorway, which is very likely to have been carved and designed by masons from Wells Cathedral (see chapter 6). The small town, or large village, is spacious and elegant, with a number of double-fronted Georgian and Victorian houses enclosing a square of orchards and gardens, and a little stream. Although there is no longer a market

St Margaret's Hospital, Taunton.

there is a surprisingly comprehensive range of shops, reflecting the popular residential character of the place and the old-fashioned self-sufficiency of this sort of rural community. Local farmhouse Cheddar and Caerphilly cheeses and Somerset 'scrumpy' are advertised at the roadside.

WELLINGTON
Early closing Thursday.

The second town in the Vale of Taunton Deane, Wellington is surrounded by rich countryside. It has now been bypassed so the main street, with several good Georgian facades, can again be enjoyed. Wellington grew up as a market town with a flourishing clothmaking industry. The building of the Bridgwater to Tiverton canal in the early nineteenth century, and the railway later in that century, helped to boost local trade. See chapter 6 for the church and chapter 8 for the museum.

Arthur Wellesley, the victorious general at the battle of Talavera, took the name of the town as his title when he became a viscount in 1808, and he went on to become the first Duke of Wellington. It is said that it was chosen for him by his family as being nearest to the family name. The monument on the Blackdown Hills overlooking the town commemorates the Duke and his victory at Waterloo (see chapter 9).

WELLS
Early closing Wednesday; market days Wednesday morning and Saturday.

As well as the magnificent cathedral and Bishop's Palace (chapter 7), the town of Wells is well worth exploring. The Market Place, under the scrutiny of the Bishop through the gateway called the 'Bishop's Eye', is an irregular L-shape. It is dominated by the Market House (now the post office) and the Town Hall, which also houses the tourist information office. The fine row of houses with shops below, on the north side, appears to be eighteenth-century from the facades, but if you look up into one of the top-floor rooms at night when they are lit up you can see the original fifteenth-century roof timbers. The Market Place and the main street contain most of the large hotels, including the Swan, the Red Lion and the Crown, and a good variety of shops. There are numerous buildings of architectural interest, including an extraordinarily large number of almshouses. St Cuthbert's church has a magnificently restored painted ceiling, with angels, crests, foliage and animals (see chapter 6).

There is a small theatre called the Little Theatre and a cinema (notice the superb Art Deco coloured glass and wall panels). The cathedral offers a wide variety of concerts and recitals throughout the year. See also Wells Cathedral (chapter 6) and Wells Museum (chapter 8). Wells makes an ideal centre from which to explore the whole county.

WINCANTON
Early closing Thursday.

The town's connection with modern horse racing is well known and the fine racecourse where National Hunt meetings are held regularly during the season is on the hill outside the town. Perhaps less well known is its historic link with the horses that hauled the Royal Mail and travellers' coaches from London to the West Country. Midway between London and Plymouth, Wincanton has been the traditional resting place and remounting point on the main road since the eighteenth century. At one time seventeen coaches a day stopped in the town, and evidence of the hospitality then offered to passengers can still be seen in the magnificent coaching inns on either side of the High Street. The Dolphin, established in 1774, the Red Lion and the Bear are good examples with grand arched entrances on to cobbled yards with adjoining stables and tack rooms.

In 1688 William of Orange stopped in Wincanton on his way from Torbay to London. He is said to have stayed in the manor house called The Dogs (with a carved dog's head over the door) on Tout Hill. The first blood of the Revolution was shed here when William's troops were attacked by a party of James II's dragoons.

An unusual effigy in the churchyard was erected by Nathaniel Ireson to himself. He was a local builder and potter; some of his fine blue and white tin-glazed pots can be seen in the Victoria and Albert Museum. The base of his effigy is decorated with the tools of his trade. In 1748 he added a new chancel to the church at his own expense. He also built Stourhead Mansion (just over the border in Wiltshire, now owned by the National Trust).

The main industry of the town was originally weaving, and evidence of the craftsmen's workshops can be seen in the elongated windows at first or second floor level in some of the older cottages. In the eighteenth century there were more than eighty looms working in the town making the material used for mattress ticking. Since then, with competition from the North of England and abroad, the industry has declined and Wincanton has not regained its former prosperity. Despite that, there is a charm and fascination in its steep streets and back alleys, with their many small antique shops and occasional views over Blackmoor Vale.

WIVELISCOMBE
The name is pronounced Wivel-is-cum but is

The Market Place, Wells.

usually shortened to 'Wivvy' locally. It is a market town serving the extensive surrounding agricultural community. Its position has been of some importance for many centuries, as pre-Roman, Roman and Saxon remains have been found, including fortifications. Castle Hill to the east of the town was the site of an early British encampment and still gives commanding views of the neighbourhood. The town was also a favourite haunt of many of the bishops of Bath and Wells, and the entrance to their 'palace' can still be seen in Church Street.

The Square is the commercial centre of Wiveliscombe and, with the High Street to the south, also contains most of the important buildings of architectural and historical interest. The architecture is varied, with the Georgian houses of Church Street giving way to the small vernacular buildings along Russells and Rotten Row. An unusual, red tile-hung building in the Square, known as the Court House but now the public library, was constructed in 1881; it has marvellously carved grotesque corbels and panels depicting mythical animals, stylised fruit and figures.

YEOVIL
Early closing Thursday; market days Monday and Friday.

Yeovil is a prosperous and expanding town at the south-east corner of Somerset, with a wide range of manufacturing industries. Yeovil has emerged from being an historic market town, with peripheral associated light industries, to a place of some considerable importance as a commercial and industrial centre.

Glovemaking was well established in Yeovil as early as the fourteenth century, probably because of the plentiful supply of skins from the sheep of the Mendip Hills and the Dorset Downs. Although the industry still continues in the town, it is declining in importance and now predominantly uses imported skins; many firms have specialised in fashion gloves and gloves for sportsmen. The Westland Aircraft Company is now the town's largest employer. This firm started during the First World War and went on to build such famous planes as the Spitfire, Seafire and Lysander. Since 1950 Westlands have also made helicopters.

Although the town's first charter was granted in 1209, little remains of ancient Yeovil; a series of fires in the middle ages and extensive modern road improvements and other developments have removed most of the visual evidence. The church of St John the Baptist, set in a quiet space amidst shops and offices, has a thirteenth-century crypt below the chancel. The early fifteenth-century tower is sturdy and impressive. The museum contains an unusual collection of firearms, a display of period costumes and archaeological finds from the area (see chapter 8). The town today offers excellent amenities, shops, entertainments and sporting facilities.

Itineraries for motorists

East and North Somerset: Taunton, A358 to Bishop's Lydeard, minor road to West Bagborough and Lydeard Hill, minor roads across the Quantocks to Bridgwater, A38 to Burnham-on-sea, A38 to Axbridge, A371 to Cheddar, A371 and byroad to Wookey, minor road to Wells, A39 to Glastonbury, Street, A39 and A361 to Burrowbridge, Taunton.

South and East Somerset: Taunton, A358 to Hatch Court, A358 and A303 to Ilminster, A358 to Chard, A30 to Cricket St Thomas, Crewkerne, B3165 and A3088 to Montacute, A3088 to Yeovil, A359 to Castle Cary, B3153 to Somerton and Langport, A378 and A358 to Taunton.

Exmoor and West Somerset: Taunton, A361 to Wiveliscombe, minor roads to Clatworthy, and minor roads and B3190 to Wimbleball

Lake, B3190 and minor road to Dulverton, B3223 and minor road to Tarr Steps, minor road and B3223 to Simonsbath (Lynton), A39 to Porlock, Selworthy, Minehead, Dunster, A39 and B3191 to Watchet, B3191 to Williton, A39 to East Quantoxhead, Nether Stowey, Bridgwater, A38 to Taunton.

Castles and abbeys: Glastonbury, A39 to Wells, A371 to Shepton Mallet, A37 and minor road to Downside Abbey, B3139 and A366 to Kilmersdon and Farleigh Hungerford, A366 and B3109 and A361 to Frome, A361 and minor road to Nunney Castle, A359 and minor road to King Alfred's Tower, B3081 to Wincanton, A303 and minor road to Cadbury Castle, A303, A372 and minor road to Muchelney Abbey, minor roads to Langport, B3153 to Somerton, B3151 to Street, A39 to Glastonbury.

The Quantock Hills from Vellow.

13
Tourist information centres

Bridgwater: Town Hall, High Street, Bridgwater. Telephone: 0278 427652 (summer only).

Burnham-on-Sea: Berrow Road, Burnham. Telephone: 0278 787852.

Cartgate: A303 Picnic and Rest Area. Major information display which is occasionally manned during the summer.

Chard: Guildhall, Fore Street, Chard. Telephone: 0640 67463 (summer only).

Cheddar: The Library, Union Street, Cheddar. Telephone: 0934 742769.

Cheddar Gorge: Cliff Street (summer only).

Dulverton: Exmoor National Park Centre, Exmoor House, Dulverton. Telephone: 0398 23665 (summer only).

Dunster: Exmoor National Park Centre, Steep Car Park, Dunster. Telephone: 0643 821835 (summer only).

Exmoor: National Park Centre, County Gate, Countisbury, North Devon. Telephone: 05987 321 (summer only).

Frome: Cattle Market Car Park, Frome. Telephone: 0373 67271 (summer only).

Glastonbury: 1 Marchant Buildings, Northload Street, Glastonbury. Telephone: 0458 32954 (summer only).

Ilminster: Shrubbery Hotel Car Park, Station Road, Ilminster. Telephone: 04605 5294 (summer only).

Minehead: The Parade, Minehead. Telephone: 0634 2624.

Shepton Mallet: Petticoat Lane, Shepton Mallet. Telephone: 0749 5258 (summer only).

Somerset Visitor Centre: Sedgemoor Services, M5 motorway (between exits 21 and 22). Telephone: 093472 883.

Taunton: The Library, Corporation Street, Taunton. Telephone: 0823 74785.

Watchet: Information obtainable from: 6 Swain Street, Watchet. This is not an official tourist information centre.

Wellington: Wellington Museum, 28 Fore Street, Wellington. Telephone: 082347 4747 (summer only).

Wells: Town Hall, Market Place, Wells. Telephone: 0749 72552.

Wincanton: The Library, 7 Carrington Way, Wincanton. Telephone: 0963 32173.

Yeovil: Johnson Hall, Hendford, Yeovil. Telephone: 0935 22884.

Yeovilton: Fleet Air Arm Museum, RNAS Yeovilton, near Yeovil. Telephone: 0935 841083 (summer only).

SOMERSET

* Country park, etc. (Chapter 2)
⊓ Archaeological site (Chapter 3)
C Castle (Chapter 5)
A Monastic building (Chapter 5)
+ Church (Chapter 6)
▲ House and garden (Chapter 7)
M Museum (Chapter 8)
O Other attraction (Chapter 9)
T Custom and tradition (Chapter 10)
■ Town or village (Chapter 11)

Down
Tropical Bird
Garden

M5
Charterhouse∏
✱Velvet Bottom
Axbridge M■ ✱Black Rack
○ ○■Cheddar
Ambleside Aviaries

ean
sure Park

Chewton
Cheese
Dairies

Farleigh
Hungerford
C+
■
○ Norwood
Farm

✱Ammerdown
Nature Trail

T East Brent
∏ Brent Knoll
BURNHAM
ON SEA
T Highbridge

Draycott
○ Chapel
Allerton
Windmill
✱
Draycott
Sleights

+ ✱Wedmore
T

∏ Priddy
T

✱ Ebbor Gorge

○ Wookey Hole

Downside Abbey

Whatley
Vineyard
+ Mells
○

+
Leigh upon
Mendip
C

+M
■FROME

Nunney
Castle

○ New Road
Farm
Peat Moors
Visitor Centre

∏ Westhay
A∏ Meare

North Wootton○
Vineyard

Wraxall
Vineyard○
○ Pilton Manor
Vineyard

+T Shepton
■ Mallet
+ East Somerset
Railway

+MT▲
■ WELLS

MO
■BRIDGWATER

○Moorlynch Vineyard

✱∏AM
TO ■GLASTONBURY
MT
T Walton ■ Street
∏ Ponter's Ball

+ Evercreech
M

○ Battle of Sedgemoor
○ Westonzoyland
North
Petherton   + ○Othery

The Moors ✱ Dundon Beacon

■ Bruton

○• King Alfred's
Tower

M■ Castle Cary

Maunsel
House

○ High Ham
Windmill

▲ Hadspen House
Wincanton
■

English
sket Centre ○
Willows ○
Wetlands
sitor Centre ∏

West Sedgemoor
Reserve ○
✱ ■ Langport

▲
Midelney
Manor

■Somerton

▲Lytes Cary

M Sparkford Motor Museum
∏ South Cadbury

A Muchelney

○ Fleet Air Arm Museum Templecombe

East Lambrook
Manor ▲
Barrington Court ▲
Stoke-sub-
Hamdon Priory A

Ilchester ■
∏

▲ Tintinhull
House

Montacute House
▲
✱ Ham Hill
M ▲ Brympton
D'Evercy

+M
■YEOVIL

Castle
Neroche
C +■ Ilminster

○ Perry's T Hinton
Cider St George

East +
Coker

○ Hornsbury Mill
■CHARD ▲○

+■Crewkerne
○ Higher Folly Farm

▲
Clapton Flour Mill

T Tatworth
Clapton Court Gardens
Cricket St Thomas
Wildlife Park

Index

Page numbers in italic refer to illustrations